European Security
in the Nuclear Age

European Security
in the Nuclear Age

James H. Wyllie

Basil Blackwell

© James H. Wyllie 1986

First published 1986

Basil Blackwell Ltd
108 Cowley Road, Oxford OX4 1JF, UK

Basil Blackwell Inc.
432 Park Avenue South, Suite 1503,
New York, NY 10016, USA

British Library Cataloguing in Publication Data

Wyllie, James H.
European security in the nuclear age.
1. Security, International   2. Nuclear
weapons — Europe   3. Europe —
Strategic aspects
I. Title
358'.39'094   VA646

ISBN 0–631–14346–7
ISBN 0–631–14347–5 Pbk

Library of Congress Cataloging in Publication Data

Wyllie, James H.
European security in the nuclear age.

Bibliography: p.
Includes index.
1. Europe — National security.   I. Title.
UQ646.W96   1986   355'.03304   85–30782
ISBN 0–631–14346–7
ISBN 0–631–14347–5 (pbk.)

Typeset by Oxford Publishing Services, Oxford
Printed in Great Britain by Billing & Sons Ltd, Worcester

Contents

Preface

This book is intended as a guide to European security arrangements. It attempts to explain why these arrangements are the way they are and why it is unlikely, and perhaps even undesirable, that there will be any radical change to them in the foreseeable future.

In recent years the 'interested public' in these matters of international security has expanded considerably in both the East and the West. This is a healthy development and is to be welcomed. The importance of issues such as the viability of nuclear deterrence, East–West arms control, and the threats posed to international security by crises and conflicts in the developing world, is clear to all. It is vital that such issues be debated in an open and informed manner. What is also crucial is that participants in the great debate – governments, civil servants, the military, scholars, students, members of the medical and scientific professions, journalists, peace campaign activists and many others – have a clear understanding of the realities of, and of the fundamental constraints imposed by, the security environment in which states operate. In the world today Europe is the centre of the public debate about international security, and the security environment of Europe is the focus of this book.

While the defence debate in Europe is to be welcomed, one depressing feature of it has been the pessimism of much of the discussion and many of the assertions. If one lives in the Middle East, Central America, or south-west Asia, then there may be profound regional reasons for widespread pessimism. But in Europe security, as defined by the absence of war, has rarely been more stable in the postwar era. Problems abound and uncertainties persist, but none of these looks like igniting a conflagration which will engulf the European continent. This book is not complacent, but it hopes to put into context and perspective some of the alarmism circulating in Europe about the prospects of war and the health of European security arrangements.

I am grateful to Professor Paul Wilkinson of the University of Aberdeen, and Professor Peter Nailor of the Royal Naval College, Greenwich, for their encouragement and support during the preparation of this book. My thanks are also due to Michael Sheehan and David Scrivener, colleagues in the Department of Politics and International Relations at the University of Aberdeen, who discussed and debated with me many of the issues contained herein. However, I alone am responsible for the book's content, and for any errors of fact or judgement.

James H. Wyllie
Aberdeen

Abbreviations

ABM	anti-ballistic missile
ASW	anti-submarine warfare
BMD	ballistic missile defence
BNW	battlefield nuclear weapon
CBMs	confidence-building measures
CDE	Conference on Confidence and Security-Building Measures and Disarmament in Europe (Stockholm)
CDU/CSU	Christian Democratic Union/Christian Social Union
CMEA	Council for Mutual Economic Assistance (also known as COMECON)
CND	Campaign for Nuclear Disarmament
CPSU	Communist Party of the Soviet Union
CSBMs	confidence- and security-building measures
CSCE	Conference on Security and Cooperation in Europe
DEFCON	Defence Readiness Condition
END	European Nuclear Disarmament
ET	emerging technology
FBS	forward-based systems
FDP	Free Democratic Party
FRG	Federal Republic of Germany
GDR	German Democratic Republic
GLCM	ground-launched cruise missile
ICBM	intercontinental ballistic missile

IGB	inner-German border
IISS	International Institute for Strategic Studies
INF	intermediate nuclear force(s)
MAD	mutual assured destruction
M(B)FR	Mutual (and Balanced) Force Reduction
MIRV	multiple independently targetable re-entry vehicle
MRV	multiple re-entry vehicle
NGA	NATO guideline area
NPT	Non-Proliferation Treaty
PRC	People's Republic of China
RDF	Rapid Deployment Force
RIIA	Royal Institute of International Affairs
RUSIJ	*Journal of the Royal United Services Institute for Defence Studies*
SAC	Strategic Air Command
SALT	Strategic Arms Limitation Talks
SDI	Strategic Defence Initiative
SLBM	submarine-launched ballistic missile
SPD	Social Democratic Party (FRG)
SSBN	ballistic-missile nuclear submarine
TNF	theatre nuclear forces
WP	Warsaw Pact

1

Forty Years of Security

In 1970 there was a mood of optimism and confidence among the foreign policy elites and the general public of the Western democracies. President Nixon had initiated the era of negotiations and, despite the continuing bloody war in south-east Asia, there appeared to be an awareness on both sides of the Iron Curtain that the blocs, led by their respective superpowers, had to coexist rather than confront. Between 1970 and 1975 the Ostpolitik treaties and the Quadripartite Agreement on Berlin considerably reduced tension in central Europe, and the German question was normalized for the foreseeable future. In May 1972 SALT I was signed and a crude nuclear parity between the United States and the Soviet Union acknowledged. The Mutual Force Reduction talks in Vienna began in 1973, and the parallel CSCE (Conference on Security and Cooperation in Europe) process yielded the Helsinki Final Act in 1975. In this period trade and cultural relations between East and West reached new postwar peaks. In diplomatic and military terms Europe was content and quiescent, and both the elites and the public seemed reassured about their security.

Within five years of the Helsinki Final Act the situation appeared to have reversed itself. The late 1970s and the 1980s have witnessed an unprecedented surge of anxiety and concern in many West European countries over the prospects for peace and security in Europe. The West European experience has been repeated in the United States, where, to an extent not seen since the heyday of the anti-Vietnam War movement, strong and vocal

pressure groups have drawn the attention of the public to issues
of national security.

In Europe there is a plethora of transnational and national
movements, most of which identify, in the first instance, the
presence of weapons, especially nuclear weapons, as the root
cause of conflict and the gravest threat to peace. Such groups
eschew the argument that it is political conflict which determines
the use of weapons, and that the nuclear weapons are not the
cause of East–West conflict but an instrument of policy. The
European Nuclear Disarmament (END) movement calls for East
Europeans to expel Soviet military bases and for West Europeans
to expel United States military bases. The superpowers are
identified as the vehicles of contemporary militarism. If they are
expelled, then somehow Europe west of the Soviet Union is
guaranteed peace, and the threat of nuclear destruction and
devastation is removed. It is the aim of END, and the national
movements such as the British Campaign for Nuclear Disarmament (CND), to transform the system of European security as it
stands and experiment with models which ignore the immutable
strategic, political and economic interests of both the nuclear
superpowers in Europe.[1]

The aims of such movements are very different from those of
the security radicals such as Olof Palme, Lords Zuckerman and
Carver, Robert McNamara and David Owen, who wish to
renovate the extant system and make it more stable and more
secure. END wants to remove nuclear weapons from Europe
altogether, unravel the Yalta agreements and return Europe to a
continent of independent sovereign states, and institute a nuclear
free zone from Portugal to Poland. In Britain CND is against any
nuclear weapons on British soil or British waters, including
British weapons, and supports a large cut in arms spending. On
the CND's coat tails in Britain a number of specialist pressure
groups with similar anxieties and objectives have evolved.
Because of their special expertise and interest these groups have
added a certain legitimacy to the Peace Movement's activities.
Such groups include Scientists Against Nuclear Arms and the
Medical Campaign Against Nuclear Weapons; the latter has
large numbers of doctors and nurses 'affronted by what they see
to be the attempt by government to involve them directly in its

nuclear war planning'.[2] And Journalists Against Nuclear Extermination feel that the media is not tackling the nuclear realities of the age properly.

North-west Europe is the major arena of activity for the Peace Movement, especially in the Federal Republic of Germany and the Netherlands as well as in Britain. The Churches are playing a novel and high profile role in Europe, helping to sustain the transnational imagery of the Movement, particularly in a divided Germany. The Protestant Churches appeal to both German states and provide a cultural bridge between them around which the young in particular can coalesce. The Protestant Church in the German Democratic Republic is against nuclear weapons and, with its stress on individual responsibility, is influencing the youth. The East German government does its best to discourage the activities of the Church in this issue.

Peace Movement activists form a small proportion of the population in the Federal Republic of Germany. Only 5 to 6 per cent at most are in the Movement, and even with sympathizers 'they still represent as a fraction no more than the communist (PCF) voters in France, i.e. less than twenty per cent.'[3] Nevertheless, the huge street demonstrations have aroused considerable media interest and drawn public attention to the issues on the agenda. The Krefeld appeal of 1982 against the Schmidt government's support of the NATO intermediate nuclear force (INF) decision gathered 1.5 million signatures. A number of books critical of current security arrangements have found a large market in North America and Europe, even though some 'generate more heat than light'.[4] Many of the popular books available to the public are action-orientated rather than providing careful analysis and unambiguously accurate information. Most tend to advance a particular normative or political line. It is of concern that such literature does not reflect the complexities of nuclear reality, but it does fuel the debate, create interest and broaden the involvement of the general public. This in turn impels policy-makers to pay more heed to the better-informed, constructive and innovative ideas about security.

A sure sign that the defence establishment is concerned about the upsurge of interest in, and anxiety about, security topics among the public of the West was the theme of the annual conference at The Hague of the much respected International Institute for Strategic Studies (IISS) in 1982: 'Defence and Consensus: The Domestic Aspects of Western Security'. Here some of the foremost defence thinkers and policy-makers addressed their peers on the importance of domestic support for defence policies, and the causes of current anxiety. Of course, even before late 1982, the feeling of some sections of the public over European security arrangements had been made manifest in increasing membership of the Peace Movement, in the sometimes massive public demonstrations in north-west Europe, and in the resolve of committed groups such as the Greenham Common peace women who had camped outside the cruise missile base for many long weary months. In a world of media competition, such 'happenings' make excellent copy and images.

Defence issues now are even more complex than in the dangerous days at the height of the Cold War. It is a difficult subject to organize intellectually and to communicate to a wider public. The technological strides of recent years, the inevitable resource allocation issues, the intrusion of the North–South question into East–West affairs, and uncertainty in some people's eyes as to who constitutes the real enemy, further hamper intellectual consideration of defence and the public's comprehension. One senior British politician, who held the post of both Defence Secretary and later Foreign Secretary during the peak of the Peace Movement's activities in the 1980s, has commented:

> There is no doubt that defence in all its complexity and sophistication, is today a very difficult subject for the politician to present simply, comprising as it does a matrix of threat and counter threat, capability and counter capability, but never offering any guarantee that ultimately war can be prevented or won, or that any level of defence effort can render one's own security invulnerable.[5]

After over forty years of learning to live with the bomb, and while most of the voting public in the West have a high degree of trust in their policy-makers, a small, vocal minority have chosen to resurrect many of the defence questions and dilemmas of twenty years ago and raise a few new issues in this complex area of human affairs. Undoubtedly, the Peace Movement has had an effect on European politics over the past few years.[6] In Britain, the Labour Party was tempted to take some of the Peace Movement's philosophy and objectives on board its 1983 election manifesto, and some would argue that this was a major contribution to its defeat in June 1983. Indeed, the drift of the Labour Party in that direction was one of the major reasons for the foundation of the British Social Democratic Party which, in alliance with the Liberal Party, split the anti-Conservative vote in Britain, allowing the Thatcher administration a huge parliamentary majority and a second term in office on only about 40 per cent of the votes cast. In the Federal Republic of Germany, the nuclear energy and closely related nuclear weapons questions severely unsettled the governing Social Democratic/Federal Democratic Party coalition throughout 1981 and 1982, and may well have contributed to the Social Democrats' poor electoral performance in March 1983. Again in north-west Europe, coalition politics in Holland and Belgium have been made even more difficult than hitherto by the nuclear weapons issue. All this political activity, much of it emanating from concern over security in Europe, encourages some policy-makers in the United States to view the West Europeans as soft on defence matters, especially over INF. This poses a further threat to West–West relations within NATO.

The actions of the Peace Movement and the reactions of the political establishments in West Europe have meant that high-profile initiatives in arms control have become a political necessity. The need for trans-Atlantic relations to be more discreetly conducted and for policy pronouncements to be more in tune with European sensitivities has been recognized, though not always successfully practised. Senior policy-makers in the field of security can no longer assume a docile public. By 1982 the public agitation evident in Europe over some defence issues began to manifest itself in the United States. The US protest movements lack the specific anxieties of the Europeans such as the concern over INF, but there is a general feeling that the arms race is getting out of control, that domestic harmony and stability are being threatened by ever-increasing defence budgets, that the United States is in danger of becoming over-defended at too high a cost, and that a dramatic gesture is required to stimulate arms control and ease East–West tensions.

On 12 June 1982 750,000 people gathered in Central Park, New York, in support of nuclear disarmament – the largest political rally in American history. A nuclear arms freeze resolution was put on the ballot papers of eight states in the mid-term elections in November 1982, and passed by 195 city councils. Notable national Democratic Party figures such as Walter Mondale and Edward Kennedy supported the freeze argument, and Kennedy co-authored a book propounding the case. Public opinion polls said that 72 per cent of Americans favoured a freeze.[7] The House of Representatives Foreign Affairs Committee in the United States Congress supported the freeze proposal sponsored by Senators Kennedy (Democratic, Mass.) and Hatfield (Republican, Maine) for a 'mutual and verifiable freeze on testing, production and further deployment of nuclear warheads, missiles and other delivery systems'.[8] Seventeen senators and 122 House members supported the proposal when it was submitted to Congress in March 1982.[9] After intense lobbying an administration sponsored counter-proposal just won the day in August, when the House of Representatives supported it by 204 votes to 202.

> The roots of this movement seem similar to those in Europe: a rising fear of nuclear war, arising from what the movement perceives to be a dangerous uncontrolled escalation in the nuclear arms race, and the statements of Reagan and his associates about limited nuclear war. It is still a minority movement and its activists are educated, but it seems to be attracting some grass roots support. American public moods about foreign policy have always had large elements of dissent and strong emotional conviction. The beginnings of the new peace movement have both. It could go far.[10]

The momentum of the freeze movement in the United States has been stalled and side-tracked since 1983, perhaps deliberately, by the introduction of the Strategic Defence Initiative (SDI), popularly known as 'Star Wars', into the defence debate. The Reagan administration argues that SDI addresses many of the weaknesses of deterrence about which the Peace Movement is worried. While this may be the intention, many defence radicals, and conservatives, perceive SDI as technologically infeasible, yet posing a severe threat to the mutual deterrence balance between the superpowers by raising the prospect of even limited protection for one superpower while the other remains vulnerable.

As in north-west Europe, an interesting feature of the Peace Movement in the United States is the deep involvement of the Churches. For instance, Archbishop Raymond Hunthausen of Seattle urged people to withhold part of their income tax as a protest against defence expenditures, and the Reverend Theodore Hesburgh, President of the University of Notre Dame, has described the nuclear threat as the world's biggest problem to which nothing could compare.[11] The American Churches, after thirty years of neglecting the issue, are paying heed to the ethical aspects of nuclear deterrence, brought out by many of the same considerations as are prevalent in north-west Europe. The Catholic bishops of the United States issued a pastoral letter in 1982 after internal and often public debate, reluctantly accepting nuclear deterrence, but only if there was meaningful progress on arms control. The federal government felt obliged to influence the process: Navy Secretary John Lehman wrote a letter to the *Wall Street Journal* expressing fears that the likely recommendations of the Catholic bishops letter, such as no first use of nuclear weapons, 'could lead directly to immoral consequences'.[12] As one would expect, the Protestant view in the United States is much more fragmented, but there is considerable sympathy for the Peace Movement: for example, the United Methodist Church (9.5 million members) telegrammed support to the Catholic bishops during their deliberations in 1982. While the Peace Movement in north-west Europe and, to a lesser extent, in the United States, does not have significant electoral support, and there is little likelihood that the more radical of their proposals, especially in Europe, will be implemented in the foreseeable future, the movement is widespread as never before, with its roots in many of the institutions of Western society. It is equally unlikely that the new public attention devoted to defence issues will fade away as it did twenty years ago. Media attention is much more intense, and the strategic, political, technological and economic agenda of defence is much longer and is developing apace, as the debate over SDI demonstrates.

This explosion of interest in high security matters is not unique in the postwar world. North-west Europe, from roughly 1955 to 1963, was the scene of vocal agitation about the dangers and risks of nuclear defence. In Britain the CND was founded, with such notable participants as Michael Foot, later leader of the Labour Party from 1979 to 1983, and the eminent historian A.J.P. Taylor. While the public as a whole never took to the cause, detailed discussion of nuclear security, especially the ethics of the issue, received considerable public exposure. As now, the Federal Republic of Germany was the scene of protests similar to those in Britain. There was widespread opposition to the siting of nuclear weapons in the Federal Republic and the equipping of the Bundeswehr with nuclear-capable missiles, despite the warheads remaining under US control: the *Kampf dem Atomtod* (struggle against atomic death) received considerable media attention. But as elections have demonstrated in the 1980s, the vast majority of the public in the Western democracies is not with the Peace Movement. The continued electoral success of the Christian Democratic/Christian Social Union in West German politics, and the decision of the SPD to cast off its pacifist and quasi-Marxist mantle in pursuit of electoral office, at Bad Godesberg in 1959, robbed the Movement of any credible political platform.[13] The West German electorate much preferred rehabilitation and prosperity in the western part of old Germany through membership of NATO and other Western institutions, to a disarmed, reunified, perhaps pro-Moscow Germany nestling uneasily between two blocs. That was the case in the darker days of the Cold War and, despite the reassertion of some of the old values of the Peace Movement of the 1950s, it is still the case today for the majority of West Germans. Elsewhere in the West the Peace Movement received little political support. In the 1960s the shock of the Cuban missile crisis and the subsequent early days of *détente* which produced the Partial Test Ban Treaty in 1963, the Non-Proliferation Treaty in 1968, and the beginning of the SALT process, all submerged the Movement's appeal. By 1970 the Peace Movement of the previous decade was of little political significance in West European politics.

It seems that a coincidence of events and decisions in the second half of the 1970s crystallized interest in many facets of European security, and disturbed the consensus and trust between public and policy-makers. This crumbling away of trust has taken place against a backdrop of the worst economic recession for over 50 years. The competition for scarce resources between social services and defence needs has focused interest on security issues and sharpened public awareness of some of the strategic and military issues facing Western decision-makers.

In Britain, where unilateral nuclear disarmament has never disappeared as an issue in minority radical politics, the cause received an impetus from the official and quasi-official debate over the Polaris replacement question.[14] By 1978 the decision over whether or not to replace Britain's Polaris independent strategic nuclear deterrent had to be made. Given that the hulls of the four Polaris ballistic missile nuclear submarines (SSBNs) would reach the end of their lives by the mid- to late 1990s, and that the lead-time for the construction of replacements would be about ten years, especially if submarine-based, then a decision had to be taken by the early 1980s. The debate within official and academic circles spilled over into the public domain, and contributed to the revival of the CND. British nuclear weapons have always been the focus of CND activity, and the Polaris debate provided the opportunity for the CND to preach a disarmament role for Britain, and perhaps break the apparent arms control log-jam in the international system. The decision of the Conservative government to buy the Trident missile system from the United States, to install in British-built SSBNs, added fuel to the CND fire. As the Trident missile can carry up to fourteen multiple independently targetable re-entry vehicle (MIRV) warheads, whereas Polaris carries only three multiple re-entry vehicle (MRV) warheads per missile, four SSBNs with sixteen missiles each means a five- or six-fold increase in the number of warheads in the British independent nuclear force. The question of cost also figured, at a time when the British economy was harder hit by the economic recession than most of its Western peer group. Not only would social services be at risk, but conventional defence resources would suffer in order to finance the independent strategic nuclear deterrent. In the June 1983 general election in Britain only the Conservative Party supported absolutely the procurement of the Trident system to replace Polaris.

Another precipitant of current concern was the neutron bomb controversy of 1978. In the winter of 1977–1978 the United States administration attempted to persuade its European allies to deploy the neutron bomb, a battlefield nuclear shell with low blast and enhanced radiation. Some military experts saw the system as an answer to the large Warsaw Pact tank armies. The enhanced radiation would kill or debilitate many of the tank crews in the area of the attack, while the low blast would do minimal damage to the local economic and social infrastructure, such as buildings. People could move back into the hostile area after twenty-four hours, and crops and water would not be affected. Bunkers with a three foot covering of soil would be enough to protect civilians who remained in the battle area. However, the neutron bomb was dubbed the 'capitalist bomb', and fears were expressed that it was so 'usable' that it was more likely to be implemented during a conflict, thereby blurring the nuclear/conventional distinction. In April 1978, in the face of vocal public opposition and a well orchestrated anti-neutron campaign, Chancellor Schmidt was on the point of agreeing that neutron be deployed in West Germany when President Carter undercut his position by postponing production of the neutron device, while modernizing existing weapons so that they could be adapted to neutron technology in the future. This decision was interpreted by the Peace Movement as a victory, and acted as a fillip to morale. The whole neutron bomb episode was not only a sad tale in intra-Alliance relations, but gave many in the Peace Movement the feeling that even the most powerful of the Alliance governments could be dissuaded from action by well organized and publicized protest campaigns.

Parallel with the initial broadside of the British nuclear debate, and in the wake of the neutron bomb controversy, the long and drawn-out SALT II process was brought to a conclusion. SALT II, signed in Vienna by President Brezhnev and President Carter in June 1979, had taken nearly six years to negotiate, prompting considerable public speculation as to the future of arms control and creating press comment on the pros and cons of the treaty, especially for West Europe. It was concern over the health, and analysis of the detail, of SALT II which brought many of the esoteric strategic concepts and the language of the international defence community in the West to the eyes and ears of a more general public. Despite reservations about the exclusion of the Soviet SS-20 missiles and 'Backfire' bombers from the text of the treaty, and the appendage of the cruise missile protocol, West European governments supported SALT II. The West Europeans looked forward to a SALT II which would address the 'Euro-strategic' weaknesses of SALT I. However, the United States Congress chose not to agree with the White House and Joint Chiefs of Staff, and SALT II looked like failing ratification when the invasion of Afghanistan provided President Carter with the opportunity to withdraw the treaty with only limited humiliation. But the Senate SALT hearings, often broadcast publicly and with extracts frequently transmitted on European networks, brought issues of nuclear security, and anxiety, into the living rooms of West Europe. Writing in 1981, one noted analyst summed up the influence of SALT thus: 'SALT is less of a cause of current concern than a precipitant. It has directed attention to nuclear deterrents in general. By emphasising what aspects of the nuclear bombs are being negotiated it also underscores what is being excluded, especially Soviet medium-range weapons.'[15]

In Europe the issue which has done most to raise the Peace Movement to its high public profile, and which has been the source of much anxiety for policy-makers and public alike, was the December 1979 decision by NATO to deploy 572 ground launched cruise missiles (GLCMs) and Pershing II missiles to offset the Soviet modernization of INF targeted on West Europe. Because NATO did not deploy nuclear forces which could definitely and accurately strike the Soviet Union from West Europe, it was felt, in view of United States–Soviet intercontinental strategic parity, that Soviet preponderance at INF level – particularly in the shape of the triple warhead, accurate and mobile SS–20s – might lead to United States–West European decoupling and a fissure in US extended deterrence. The prospect was raised of the Soviet intercontinental arsenal holding the US land-based intercontinental arsenal at bay while land-based Soviet INF forces blackmailed West Europe. The only forces in West Europe which could realistically threaten the Soviet homeland were the sea-based British and French independent strategic nuclear deterrents, but these were weapons of total war earmarked by the national governments for retaliation following an attack on the homelands. These independent European deterrents provide little succour for the other, non-nuclear, NATO European states, which rely for nuclear deterrence on the integrity of the United States' commitment. The most exposed and vulnerable of these states, and the one in need of most reassurance, is the Federal Republic of Germany. American weapons which could hit the Soviet Union were required in Europe in order to cement the tenuous connection between the United States nuclear defence of West Europe and the home-based US intercontinental arsenal. This was supposed to reassure the West Europeans. Indeed, the whole plan was very much the result of West European agitation and initiatives, especially by Chancellor Schmidt of the Federal Republic.

But rather than reassuring the West Europeans, the December 1979 NATO decision offered the opportunity to the Peace Movement to build upon its neutron bomb success. Since then there have been across north-west Europe widespread protest marches and gatherings, gaining considerable media attention. Part of the NATO decision was to attempt to engage the Soviet Union in arms control talks which, if successful in diminishing the perceived Soviet threat to West Europe, could result in reduced or no deployment of United States INF in Europe. The apparent reluctance of the Reagan administration to enter into arms control negotiations with the Soviet Union for nearly two years played into the hands of the Peace Movement, and became a source of serious concern to many West European governments. By late 1981 arms control negotiations had started in Geneva, but grave reservations about the seriousness of intent of the United States continued to plague the West Europeans, publics and governments alike.

A distinct anti-American bias has developed in the Peace Movement in north-west Europe, and it has two causes: one is rooted in a search for cultural tradition, and the other in qualms over United States nuclear doctrine and intentions. Amongst many of the younger generation, being pro-American means supporting the establishment and all that is perceived to be wrong with society. Amongst some there is resentment at dependence on the United States, amongst others a dislike of what they see as a preponderance of American values, be it in fashion, art, entertainment or business practice. As the West European economies have recovered and prospered in the postwar era, and a full appreciation of the reasons underlying the United States' presence recedes into history, a desire to return to a more traditional, 'innocent' Europe is manifest in the attitudes of some young Europeans. This is particularly so in Germany. The Protestant Church and many young people search for a nationwide peace movement incorporating both Germanies, and resulting in the withdrawal of all occupation troops from German soil, east and west. In the Federal Republic some sections sense diminishing sovereignty in the face of superpower rivalry (for example, in the gas pipeline issue, the Afghanistan invasion and the 1980 Olympic Games boycott) and look to radical – some would argue utopian – ideas, such as militant pacifist nationalism for the dawn of the new era. In Germany, pan-Germanism and the Peace Movement run in harness. In many minds the route to German unification and the return to the more attractive aspects of German culture and tradition lies through nuclear disarmament and the expulsion of the superpowers from central Europe. But opinion polls reveal that anti-Americanism is much less widespread than media representation suggests. In the FRG in spring 1982 the Emnid poll found that 73 per cent of respondents had a positive image of the United States, and 24 per cent a negative image. For the Soviet Union the figures were 20 per cent and 77 per cent respectively. Only 17 per cent favoured the withdrawal of United States troops.[16]

Nevertheless, in the Peace Movement anti-Americanism is a predominant emotion, and in addition to often vague cultural and political objections this strand is reinforced by the tone and direction of United States foreign policy and strategic doctrine. The same United States that wishes to secure peace in West Europe seems reluctant to engage the Soviet Union in constructive dialogue on issues such as strategic arms control and regional instabilities, and is doing its best to support military dictatorships and undermine popular reformist governments in

Latin America. *Détente*, which means so much to continental West Europeans, has been erased from the vocabulary of US foreign policy. The stridency of foreign policy in Washington seems to be matched by pronouncements and new directions in United States nuclear doctrine, particularly towards war-fighting options, with scant regard for the interests of the West Europeans.

The official changes in the strategic nuclear doctrine pronounced in the early 1980s have disturbed many people in both Europe and the United States. The Carter administration's PD59, which advanced even greater options at strategic nuclear level, enabling United States intercontinental counter-force weapons to be targeted on Europe outside the Soviet homeland, was seen by many to facilitate limited nuclear war in Europe rather than to enhance the credibility of deterrence by increasing the President's options. The fact that PD59 was merely a refinement of the 1974 Schlesinger retargeting plans, and that the United States has been slowly but surely moving for many years towards deterrence by denial of victory rather than by massive retribution, was overlooked in the tumult. As with the neutron bomb and INF, PD59 drew the attention of the public to the previously esoteric matters of nuclear doctrine and, on face value, seemed to suggest malign American intent. The Peace Movement chose to interpret the INF deployments in this light as well. The United States' GLCMs and Pershing II missiles would allow a limited nuclear war in Europe, while the American homeland could remain unscathed. This, of course, ignores the reality that GLCMs and Pershing II missiles would be striking the Soviet homeland, and the Soviets have insisted that if American nuclear weapons hit the Soviet Union it will not matter where they came from: it is those to whom they belong who will suffer retaliation. This is why the West European governments want United States INF, which locks the United States into West European defence and hence enhances the deterrence effect at that level.

The public view of this official doctrinal approach has been clouded and distracted by the unfortunate rhetoric emanating from the Reagan White House, which grabs the headlines and seems to confirm the disarmers' claims. In democracies public support for a defence strategy is essential: 'Whether a strategic doctrine is acceptable to the people for whom it has been developed is as important in an alliance of democratic societies as the doctrine's ability to impress the enemy.'[17]

Vice President George Bush is on record as having stated that nuclear war is winnable. Ed Meese, chief counsellor to President Reagan in the White House, has spoken of nuclear war as 'something that may be undesirable',[18] while Alexander Haig, when Secretary of State, raised the prospect of nuclear warning shots in the European theatre in the event of conventional conflict. In October 1981 President Reagan caused a storm by the observation that 'I could see where you could have the exchange of tactical weapons against troops in the field without bringing either one of the major powers to pushing the button.'[19] This statement strengthened both the Peace Movement's claims and public suspicions in West Europe. It implied that nuclear exchanges in Europe meant something less than 'pushing the button'. Obviously, if you lived in Germany this was not the case. The Reagan administration seemed to be unaware that what might be intended to reassure domestic opinion in the American heartland would also be picked up by West European ears. What is far away and tactical for the American public is close to home and strategic for the continental West Europeans. This is a fact of Alliance life which has plagued NATO's strategic doctrine for thirty years, and which is inherent in the INF discussion. INF tends to be sold by Washington to the American population as a nuclear adjunct to United States conventional forces in Europe, while it is packaged to the West Europeans as a solid bridge between the might of the US strategic arsenal and West European defence via deterrence. In the past this doctrinal fudge has held because administrations, in Washington and elsewhere, treated it sensitively, and the public eye was not securely fixed upon it.

The simultaneous insistence by the Reagan White House, and also by the Carter White House in its later years, that *détente* is moribund and that a new Cold War is upon us, has not assisted in calming anxieties. Most West European governments still see some life in *détente*, and experience some returns such as trade and closer human relations. The problem here is that the hawks in Washington use the imagery of a soft Europe to support their tough foreign policy postures and defence doctrines, while the European disarmament movement uses the rhetoric of Washington to support their views that the United States can no longer be trusted to act in the best interests of the peoples of West Europe.

In the past few years there has been particular instability in matters of strategic doctrine. The various United States statements on the possibility of a limited nuclear war in Europe, or indicating that a nuclear war might be less than a catastrophe for the United States, may have been intended to strike fear into the hearts of the Soviet leaders (and may indeed have done so), but their principal visible effect has been to cause alarm and despondency in Western Europe and in the United States herself.[20]

Further unease in West–West relations over American foreign policy actions and perceptions resulted from Washington's reactions to the Soviet invasion of Afghanistan and the imposition of martial law in Poland. Again the Washington analysis was much more pessimistic than the continental West European interpretation. There was a tendency in both the Carter and Reagan administrations to ascribe Soviet action in south-west Asia to a grand strategic design, derived from Soviet policy in Africa in the mid-1970s, to encircle the Indian Ocean periphery and drive for the Gulf oil-fields and warm-water ports. In West Europe the perception was one of Soviet opportunism when low-cost possibilities presented themselves, but it was not thought sensible to risk the *modus vivendi* in Europe for the sake of faraway crises of marginal strategic significance. The Reagan administration saw the Soviet hand behind every move by the Polish authorities against the Solidarity trade union movement, while the continental European governments were much more aware of the peculiar geostrategic and social situation of Poland, perceiving that the Polish military, acutely aware of the Soviet presence, took the action they did as much to forestall direct Soviet intervention as to act as a Soviet proxy. Not only have these divergent perceptions of the implications of such crises, and how to manage them, lowered West European confidence in American policy-making, but they have sharpened the thrust of international affairs into public life. So much has happened on the international agenda in the space of a few short years, and is receiving so much media attention, that the general public is becoming more aware of policy problems, strategic dilemmas and military vulnerabilities than it has ever been before. This is so not only in West Europe, but also in the United States.

> Under the pressure of a tight economy and government policies which reduce social services and increase military expenditures, the issues of strategic modernisation and the cost of military procurement overall have come to generate public resistance. Taken together, these two developments have begun to shake the public consensus which has supported the structure and direction of American – and Western – defence efforts in the past.[21]

The pace of defence technology, and the media attention it attracts, have also had an unsettling effect on people's peace of mind. Multiple warheads, weapons miniaturization, astounding accuracy over great distances, increasing numbers and expense, have all introduced a new psychological dimension into public anxieties. The INF issue, the capabilities of the GLCM, Pershing II, and SS-20, and the prospect of an arms race in space raised by SDI – all confirm many of the forebodings about high technology and appear to vindicate fears of the scientific manipulation of mankind. On the European continent the Peace Movement draws much of its strength from the ecology movement, centred on the struggle against nuclear energy power plants. In the Federal Republic of Germany, where the 'Greens', the party-political manifestation of the ecology movement, have gained a limited degree of political success, the Peace Movement and the ecology movement have more or less merged, and are often described as *Okofriedensbewegung* (Ecopeace).[22]

Even though in Europe the majority of the electorate do not support the Peace Movement, there are feelings of vulnerability among sections of the West European populations not experienced since the balance of terror days of the late 1950s. As we have seen, over twenty years ago such concerns were much more the preserve of the intelligentsia and received only a fraction of the popular and political support of the present Peace Movement. The paradox is that the prospects for a disarming first strike with nuclear weapons by one superpower against the other were much more favourable in the late 1950s and early 1960s than now. Invulnerable second-strike systems, especially in the form of SSBNs, which could take retribution in the event of a first strike, began to be deployed in the early 1960s, and the hardening of missile silos to withstand blast, and the dispersal of aircraft on quick-reaction alert readiness so as not to present an easy target, came after the peace movements began to lose their appeal twenty years ago. In the early 1960s the incentives for a first strike, especially for the United States which was still relatively invulnerable, were less unattractive than today. At that time there was the prospect of removing the other superpower from the international power balance at minimal cost to your own homeland. In the late 1980s such a situation no longer pertains, and has not done so for many years. The SSBN fleets present a high possibility of devastating nuclear response to any use of nuclear weapons aiming to cripple the strategic power of the other superpower or threaten the security of major allies. Whatever notions may persist in some of the more conservative defence circles in the United States about 'windows of vulnerability', it would be dangerous to assume that the United States would not use its superior SSBN fleet to respond to a successful disarming first strike by Soviet heavy land-based missiles on the American intercontinental ballistic missile (ICBM) force. In all likelihood some accurate American land-based ICBMs would survive to pose a threat of limited retaliation, but even if not the scale of devastation would be such that it is difficult to imagine any American president not using some of the submarine launched ballistic missile (SLBM) force – which is becoming increasingly accurate as Trident comes into service – to make an appropriate response. The superpower intercontinental nuclear arms balance is much more stable in the 1980s than it was in the late 1950s and 1960s.

Indeed, twenty-five years ago there was much more cause for concern in Europe. Not only was the strategic nuclear power relationship of the superpowers unstable, but there was an intra-European crisis which threatened war: the status of Berlin was in dispute between the occupying powers. The Soviet Union wished to oblige the West to recognize the Soviet zone of Germany as the state of the German Democratic Republic. To have done so would have undercut the West's commitment to German reunification, which was the *sine qua non* for the Federal Republic of Germany's membership of NATO. On two occasions between 1958 and 1961 the Soviet Union threatened to conclude a separate peace treaty with the East Germans if the West did not transfer to the East German government responsibility for access routes to West Berlin across the Soviet zone. The Western Allies indicated that they would refuse to acknowledge East German control.

This period was the one of the 'missile gap' when, following Sputnik, there was a genuine fear that the Soviet Union had rushed ahead with ICBM production and achieved a degree of nuclear superiority; certainly, Soviet behaviour and language did everything to encourage this view. The missile gap myth was not to be revealed until 1961 or 1962. Throughout the years 1958 to 1961 the atmosphere in Berlin was tense, and the Western zones received conventional military reinforcement. The Eisenhower and Khrushchev summit meeting of 1960 in Paris was cancelled owing to the animosity and distrust created by the U-2 incident, when an American spy plane was shot down over the Soviet Union in May 1960. In June 1961 a summit meeting between the young President Kennedy and Khrushchev in Vienna appeared to make East–West relations worse, not better. In August 1961 the Soviets and the East Germans built the Berlin wall, dividing the four-power-controlled city of Berlin. This stemmed the flood of refugees escaping from the Soviet zone of Germany via Berlin to the West (three million between 1949 and 1961), and completed the Iron Curtain dividing Europe. The tension continued and, in October, for two days, Soviet and American tanks faced each other with engines running at Checkpoint Charlie, on the Berlin wall, where the Soviet and American zones of the city converged. In 1961 the superpower nuclear balance was extremely sensitive, and the most tense crisis spot on the globe, with both the superpowers in attendance, was in the heart of Europe. The Cold War of rhetoric and mistrust reached a pitch never experienced since then.

West Europe is the major prize in East–West competition.

Owing to its geostrategic position, economic importance, political and military power, and its level of technological achievement and potential, West Europe is *the* vital element in the global balance of power. The combined GDP of France, Britain, the Federal Republic of Germany and Italy in 1983 far exceeded the estimated GNP of the Soviet Union. The same West European countries have over 1.5 million people in the armed services, even before mobilization,[23] and their political influence and prestige, either individually or as members of the EEC or NATO – though impossible to quantify – are considerable.

Yet actual East–West military conflict has only occurred outside the European theatre. The superpowers and their respective alliances have avoided war in Europe. Such conflicts as have erupted have been confined to the extra-European world, and in these wars the superpowers have carefully avoided combat between American and Soviet forces. In the Korean War, conflict was confined to the Korean peninsula, and although American forces were deeply involved under UNO auspices they did not fight Russians. It was the midst of the Cold War, but Chinese and North Korean forces were never joined by Soviet forces. Similarly in the Vietnam War the massive presence of American forces, over 500,000 strong at the height of United States military involvement in south-east Asia, was not challenged by Soviet military force. While considerable military and financial aid has been supplied to the superpower client states in the Middle East, and many wars have broken out there, American and Soviet forces have not entered the fray. When it looked as if there was a danger of this happening, in October 1973, Washington raised the spectre of nuclear war to dissuade the Soviets, and also to restrain the Israelis from pursuing their successful counter-offensive to the gates of Cairo. In Angola and Ethiopia in the mid- to late 1970s the military success of Cuban forces acting as Soviet proxies was not challenged by American military power. In south-west Asia in 1979, when the Soviet Union used direct and massive military force outside the borders of the Soviet bloc for the first time since 1945, the United States did not respond in kind. The invasion of Afghanistan caused great indignation and alarm in the West, but there was never any prospect of a Western military response. The fate of Afghanistan was not worth a war with the Soviet Union.

Since 1945 Europe has been a relative haven of peace. NATO has been a successful alliance: 'It has transformed one of the most volatile regions of the world – central and western Europe – into what can only be termed a zone of peace, in which the prospect of war has become remote as well as unthinkable.'[24] In West Europe NATO provides the security backdrop to economic development and cooperation. The Federal Republic of Germany seems reconciled to the German military defeat of forty years ago, the division of old Germany, the denial of nuclear weapons status, and Alliance controls on its armed forces. Soviet military and political power has been contained in Europe since the fall of Czechoslovakia in 1948 and, while there may be fears of 'Finlandization', there are no examples of any NATO or other non-Communist European state being coerced into a political or foreign policy posture similar to the Finnish experience, which is due very much to Finland's unique geostrategic situation. Indeed, it could be argued that the political processes are running in the opposite direction, if one examines the recent history and experience of Poland. In Europe military force has been used in internal domestic problems: for example, in Northern Ireland the British Army has provided aid to the civil power in an effort to keep the peace between hostile politico-religious factions. In Poland the military have been used to impose a long period of martial law in the face of popular unrest, manifested by the Solidarity trade union movement, against the Communist authorities. Military force has been used by the Soviet Union, sometimes with other East European military forces, in intra-bloc disputes within the Warsaw Pact – in East Berlin in 1953, in Hungary in 1956, and in Czechoslovakia in 1968. Such action was taken in order to sustain the Communist Party's monopoly of political power, and remove any potential threats to Soviet political and military hegemony in East Europe. However, in all these instances of the use of military force, considerable care has been taken to contain the conflicts. In particular, whatever the rhetoric of the United States about Soviet military intervention in the domestic affairs of its Communist satellites, there has never been any prospect of the US or NATO using military force to counter Soviet actions. Since 1945 European stability and security, especially in the democracies of West Europe, have been sustained. There has been no major or significant East–West crisis in Europe since the construction of the Berlin wall in 1961.

Need the West Europeans feel so vulnerable as the twentieth century draws to a close? Is Europe on the brink of cataclysmic war? Has the political, economic, military and technological environment changed so much, or is it changing so rapidly, that war in the European theatre has now become such an attractive instrument of policy that conflict between East and West in Europe is imminent or likely in the foreseeable future? An appreciation of the salient characteristics of the security relationship between East and West in Europe since 1945 will facilitate an understanding of why and how stability and security have been sustained in Europe, and allow an assessment of the major threats to this welcome condition, as perceived by the West, as we approach the end of the twentieth century.

There are three dominant characteristics in the East–West security relationship in Europe since the Second World War. First, East–West competition has been ideological in nature. Even before the end of the war against Nazi Germany it was obvious that the wartime allies which were to occupy Germany and reconstruct a war-torn Europe would be engaged in a war of ideas about the preferred political and economic direction of the new Germany and Europe. Conflicts of ideas usually produce more bitterness and much deeper hostility than competition over markets or resources. But a counter-balance to and control on the apparent inevitability of ideological competition at this time was that it would be conducted in a nuclear environment – the second factor in the postwar East–West relationship. In August 1945 the United States Air Force dropped atomic bombs on two Japanese cities, Hiroshima and Nagasaki. The effects were devastating – and war-winning in the Far East. At the time the United States had an atomic monopoly, and was itself invulnerable to retaliation. However, it was clear that the Soviet Union would make every effort to achieve atomic weapons status, and did so by 1949. By 1957, with the Soviet Union's acquisition of ICBM capability, the American homeland became vulnerable, and a gradual crude nuclear parity has subsequently evolved. In the early postwar years the might of the Red Army in central Europe held West Europe hostage to United States good behaviour, while the Soviet Union was building up its .nuclear forces. Given the prospect of the escalation from ideological rivalry to military conflict, the presence in the heart of Europe of two major powers equipped with nuclear weapons could not be ignored. There may well be other factors inhibiting recourse to a major European military conflict to advance poltical objectives, such as memories of Europe's two total wars in the twentieth century and a lingering war-weariness. However, nuclear weapons are now in Europe, and given the proclivity throughout human history for conflicts of ideas, religious and political, to spill over into military conflict, it is not unreasonable to suggest that nuclear weapons have a considerable influence on policy-makers when considering any military option.

The result of the clear political demarcation of Europe between two unyielding ideologies, liberal democracy and Soviet Communism, in a nuclear environment, is the third salient characteristic of the East–West security relationship in Europe: geopolitical accommodation and a uniquely long period of non-war in the European theatre. Since the formalization of the American defence commitment to West Europe in 1949, the ideological configuration of the European continent has not undergone any significant change, irrespective of social and political movement. Bloc security arrangements have contributed to an ossification of the political map of Europe, as well as over forty years of peace.

2

The Ideological Conflict

Competing ideological concepts on how the international system ought to be ordered have permeated East–West relations since 1943, to a degree never experienced in the inter-war years. Collapsing German military and political power in Europe in the last two years of the Second World War presented unique opportunities to the Western Allies and to the Soviet Union to extend their political and military power and influence. The paradox, of which policy-makers were well aware as the war drew to a close, was that the more successful the Soviet Union was in extending its political and military power, then the less secure its former Western Allies would feel in an uncertain postwar world, and vice versa. Following the massive German defeat on the Eastern front at Stalingrad in the winter of 1942–43, it became clear that the Allied powers of the United States, Britain and the Soviet Union would eventually gain military victory over the Axis powers of Germany, Italy and Japan. The combination of Russian military manpower and sacrifice (for example, in 1943 179 of Germany's 266 divisions were engaged on the Eastern front)[1] and the industrial might of the United States made victory for the Axis powers, given the sustained political cohesion of the Allies, inconceivable. With the change in military fortunes wrought on the Eastern front at Stalingrad, the Allied powers, particularly Britain and the Soviet Union, began to devote considerable thought to the postwar settlement.[2]

Poland, the country over whose fate Britain went to war in

1939, became the litmus test of Soviet intentions in East Europe, as the Red Army rolled westwards. Poland was special in a number of ways. First, it is on the traditional invasion route from central Europe into Russia. Through or from Poland the Russian people have suffered three invasions in the twentieth century. In the inter-war years, as a result of the Treaty of Versailles arrangements for the resurrected Polish state, and as an outcome of the Soviet–Polish war of 1920–21, large areas of foreign or imperial Russia, including parts of Byelorussia and the Ukraine dear to Moscow's heart, came under Warsaw's jurisdiction. A secret clause of the notorious Molotov–Ribbentrop Pact of August 1939 allowed for a Soviet invasion of eastern Poland following an attack by Nazi Germany in the west, and the annexation by Moscow of large parts of Poland, as well as permitting the Soviet Union a free hand in the Baltic states of Estonia, Latvia and Finland. Lithuania was to remain under German influence.[3] For reasons of security, *inter alia*, the postwar future of Poland was of the utmost importance to Stalin and the Western Allies, especially Britain, which appeared to recognize Soviet concern as quite legitimate. At the Tehran and Yalta summits, agreements were reached supporting the Polish–Soviet frontiers of 1941, even though they were the result of Nazi–Soviet collusion. However, it should be noted that in the disputed territory the Poles were outnumbered by Ukrainians and Byelorussians.[4] Postwar Poland was to be compensated with German territory to the west.[5]

But what of the political future of Poland? Would Poland, the first non-Soviet territory to experience liberation by the Red Army from the Nazi occupation, be allowed to decide its own political future? Would the Red Army be used to impose ideological conformity on liberated East Europe? Or would the Soviet Union eschew the great opportunity offered by the westward advance of the Red Army to export and sustain Soviet Communist ideology as the ruling creed in a region of Europe traditionally prone to Russian influence? The Western Allies paid particular heed to Soviet policy towards Poland, which was far removed from Western military reach and where events on the ground were well beyond Western political influence. Poland was the test-case of Soviet political intentions and, as perceived through Western eyes, of Soviet goodwill towards the West. When Poland fell before the Nazi–Soviet attack in September 1939 the Warsaw government fled to Paris, and then in 1940 to London, where it was recognized by the British government as the legitimate government in exile of Poland. The United States also recognized the legitimacy of the London Poles. Naturally, the London Poles did not recognize the legitimacy of the Soviet–Polish frontier as agreed between Molotov and Ribbentrop in 1939. In June 1941, the Soviet Union, so recently an aggressor against Poland, was attacked by Nazi Germany, and as a result found itself an ally of Britain, the protector of the London Poles. So here was the British government supporting the war effort of the Soviet Union, one of whose objectives was to expel the Nazi invader and re-establish its own 1941 frontiers. The need to sustain the wartime unity of the great powers in the Alliance obliged Churchill, and with greater reluctance Roosevelt, to accede to Stalin's territorial objectives *vis a vis* Poland, but both required of Stalin certain political guarantees of Poland's democratic future, not least for reasons of domestic politics in Britain and the United States.[6]

Before the Yalta summit of February 1945, Soviet behaviour as regards the political future of Poland had failed to reassure the Western Allies and had created deep-seated suspicion of Soviet intentions. In April 1943 Radio Berlin had announced the discovery of a mass grave containing bodies of over 10,000 Polish officers in the forest of Katyn near Smolensk. There was considerable evidence to suggest that these were the bodies of most of the 14,300 Polish officers taken prisoner by the Soviet Union in 1939, and who had since disappeared mysteriously. As a result of the discovery, Moscow broke off relations with the London Poles, and they were never resumed. In July 1944, as Soviet troops crossed the Molotov–Ribbentrop line in the offensive against the retreating Nazi armies, Stalin announced his support for a rival Polish government – in the form of a committee for the national liberation of Poland, to be based in the eastern Polish city of Lublin. The members of this Soviet-sponsored Communist Polish government, based in liberated Poland, came to be known as the 'Lublin Poles' as distinct from the 'London Poles' supported by the Western Allies. The

Lublin Poles recognized the 1941 Soviet–Polish frontiers, and signed political and military agreements with the Soviet Union. In late July and early August 1944, efforts by the London Poles to reach agreement with the Lublin Poles came to nought – the London Poles were offered only four posts in a proposed eighteen member cabinet, and the Lublin committee was determined not to budge on the frontier issue. In the eyes of the London Poles, and of the Western Allies, the most damning indictment of the Lublin Poles and their Soviet sponsors was their refusal to acknowledge the trauma of Warsaw in August and September 1944. With the approach of the Red Army to within a few miles of Warsaw, the Polish resistance, loyal to the London Poles, had risen in insurrection in the hope of expelling the Nazis and of being in a position to share the liberation of Poland's capital with the Red Army. But Stalin had stopped the Red Army on the banks of the River Vistula, and allowed the Nazis to decimate the Polish underground and the city of Warsaw. Stalin had also done his best to hinder the airlift of supplies to the Warsaw Poles by the Western Allies. When the Red Army marched into Warsaw in December 1944 it found a political as well as a social and economic vacuum.[7]

Throughout East Europe Stalin subordinated purely military to political needs, and many Soviet forces which could have been used to push directly towards Germany were directed elsewhere. Rumania surrendered and declared war on Germany in August 1944, yet none the less the Red Army occupied the whole country. The Soviet Union declared war on Bulgaria on 6 September 1944, even though Bulgaria had never been at war with the Soviet Union and was in the process of peace negotiations with the Western Allies. Of little direct strategic but of considerable political significance, Hungary was next on the agenda: there the Red Army waged a bitter campaign, particularly in the liberation of Budapest – 'the Russians were staking out a postwar sphere of influence and were willing to pay heavily for it.'[8]

At the Yalta summit Stalin promised to include a few London Poles in the Lublin government, and free elections as soon as possible, but the decision as to which parties were 'anti-fascist' and thus able to participate was in Soviet hands. Despite Stalin's support of the summit's 'Declaration on Liberated Europe', pledging 'the right of all peoples to choose the form of government under which they will live',[9] a Communist government was forced upon Rumania, and Communist and pro-Soviet factions dominated the new administrations in Bulgaria, Hungary and Czechoslovakia. In Poland sixteen leaders of the underground movement were arrested and the democratic process made a mockery.[10] As a measure of Stalin's intentions, the Western Allies could only draw the most gloomy of conclusions from the experience of liberated Poland and from Soviet behaviour throughout the rest of East Europe: 'There is a sense in which the Cold War, like World War Two, began with flesh-and-blood in Poland.'[11] While, for reasons of geo-strategic realism, the Western Allies were prepared to accept territorial adjustments to the Polish state, London and Washington were quite sincere in their concern over Poland's democratic future.

Although the Western Allies might despair over Soviet political behaviour in East Europe, in West Europe the liberating powers encouraged the re-establishment of political systems which were primarily democratic–capitalist in nature. But a major distinction between the behaviour of the Soviet Union in East Europe and the United States and Britain in West Europe was that while the Soviet Union was required to use a considerable degree of coercion to impose its preferred system in the East, this was not the case with the Allies in the West. A major exception to the Western model was Greece where, in late 1944, British forces were used to suppress a Greek Communist insurrection. By 1947 the economies of Britain, Italy, France and Greece were precariously close to bankruptcy, from which chaos it seemed only Communism or other forms of dictatorship could emerge, either through the ballot box or by *coup d'état*. But throughout West Europe, especially in France and Italy where there was a genuine fear of Communism emerging from the rubble of the war-shattered economies as the dominant political creed, the primary instrument used to implant and sustain democratic capitalism was to be American economic power. The Marshall Plan, which introduced a massive infusion of American capital into the ailing West European economies, propped up democratic-capitalism and assured a period of relative political stability.[12] In accordance with the 'universalist notion' of international security prevalent in Washington at the time, Marshall Aid was offered to the Soviet Union and the liberated East European states.[13] After some initial hesitation, the generous offer was rejected. The usual interpretation of this behaviour is that Stalin saw the extension of American capital into East Europe as a political threat to the Soviet Union, and as an attempt to project democratic capitalism to its very borders, particularly given the proclivity of some East European governments to participate.[14]

Clearly, in the concluding years of the Second World War and in the early postwar years, both the Soviet Union and the Western Allies perceived what was desirable in terms of international security and domestic socio-economic organization through an ideological prism of predetermined values and attitudes. Whether or not both camps valued the ideology they supported purely for its own sake, as embracing the true moral principles by which states ought to organize themselves given the right circumstances, or whether they cynically used ideology as a *realpolitik* device by which to demarcate respective spheres of influence, is a fascinating debate.[15] Whatever one's views on this controversy may happen to be, it is indisputable that in the period presently under discussion both camps assessed the measure of threat, in the first instance, by the actual or potential ideological characteristics of the governments and societies in question. Rhetoric and behaviour were considered to be ideologically based and motivated. Democratic-capitalist governments in East Europe were seen as inimical to Soviet political, military and economic security, just as the prospect of a Communist ascendancy in France or Italy was viewed with horror by the United States and Britain.

Ideas antithetical to one prevailing system came to be seen as a threat to its integrity and, as the fate of Poland clearly illustrates, inflexibility began to colour the relations of the former wartime Allies. The control of territory meant more than just privileged access to economic resources or the gain of military–strategic advantage: it meant the advance and projection of ideas which in turn meant the greater insulation of the respective camps from the debilitating dangers of alternative notions of societal organization. It was not language or culture or geography which fundamentally divided the Western Allies from the Soviet Union, but differing irreconcilable ideologies, the least flexible of which was Stalin's brand of Soviet Communism. According to its scientific laws, any traditional non-Communist state must, by definition, pose a threat: 'Leninism and totalitarianism created a structure of thought and behavior which made post-war collaboration between Russia and America – in any normal sense of civilized intercourse between national states – inherently impossible.'[16]

The impossibility of collaboration between adversarial ideological systems, particularly when great prizes were at stake, was nowhere more clearly demonstrated than in wartime Germany between 1945 and 1948. At Yalta it was agreed that on surrender, the country should be divided into four zones, one each to be administered by the United States, the Soviet Union, Britain and France. All four states would be members of the Allied Control Council, which would coordinate the administration and control of Germany. It was also agreed that reparations be exacted from Germany, most of which were to be received by the countries having suffered the heaviest losses. In this regard the Soviet Union was the major candidate, though the British wished to delay consideration of the exact sums to be paid. Although the dismemberment of Germany was discussed at length at Yalta, there was no definite agreement to proceed along such a course. When the war ended in May 1945 only the French, of the four occupying powers, pressed for partition; the British and the Americans were concerned about the economic burden of a dismembered Germany. The administration of Germany by the military commanders-in-chief of the occupying powers, in their own zones and answerable only to the unanimous decisions of the Control Commission for all Germany, was meant only as a practical way of running the defeated country in the period between military collapse and an overall German peace treaty. The German capital, Berlin, was likewise occupied by the four powers, with military commands supreme in their own zones except when answerable to the Berlin *Kommandatura*, also pending a German peace treaty. The

Potsdam summit conference of July/August 1945 was intended to settle the future of Germany and provide a German peace treaty around which the reorganization of Europe would fall into place.

At Potsdam there was some agreement. The three victorious powers (France was excluded from Potsdam) agreed on the demilitarization and de-nazification of Germany, on the desirability of a common economic policy for all four zones of occupation, and to begin the establishment of a German administration to carry out Allied instructions. But the Potsdam summit is better known for its disagreements than its agreements. The Soviets unilaterally ceded part of their zone to Poland to compensate for the loss to the Soviet Union of Polish territory in the east. This territory was thus removed from the area theoretically to be controlled by all four occupying powers, and the Western Allies accepted the new boundary as only provisional.

The most crucial and divisive issue at Potsdam, which was to plague the relations between the victorious powers in Germany for the next three years, was that of German reparations. Heeding the mistakes of the reparation agreements at Versailles in 1919, the Western Allies were against large cash transfers, nor did they wish to reduce living standards in Germany below an acceptable and, in their eyes, politically manageable standard. Naturally the Soviet Union, in view of the awful devastation suffered at the hands of Nazi Germany between 1941 and 1945, would be the major recipient of German reparations, and wished for as much cash, capital equipment, food, raw materials and current production as it could possibly get.[17] The whole issue of reparations was of the most vital importance to Moscow. But by the time of Potsdam, the British and Americans had reached the conclusion that, while Germany should be deprived of war-making potential, its economic and social recovery was essential to the realization of the Western vision of postwar Europe. By July 1945 the Western Allies saw reparations as an instrument of political policy in the growing ideological competition with the Soviet Union.[18] Unable to reach a final agreement on reparations the three powers at Potsdam came to a temporary compromise, pending further discussion:

The upshot at Potsdam was to leave the total reparations

bill undecided – a heavy blow to the Russians – and allow each occupying power to remove capital assets from its own zone, subject to later understandings as to overall production levels and economic policy for Germany as a whole (the Russians undertook to provide reparations to Poland; the Western powers were to care for other claimants). This one centralising element in a generally decentralising plan was given some reality, at least potentially, and the Soviet Union was given limited access to the industrial wealth of the Ruhr, by the provision that 10 per cent of the assets from the three western zones 'unnecessary for the German peace economy' (however that was to be defined) were to be given gratis to the Soviet Union and 15 per cent were to be traded to the Russians for food and raw materials from their zone.[19]

However, the agreement at Potsdam 'that during the period of military occupation Germany "would be treated as a single economic entity", and the German population would be accorded uniform treatment throughout the country',[20] was never fulfilled. France, fearful of a recovering unified Germany, objected to and obstructed centralized economic administration, while the Soviet Union, in its zone, pursued policies inimical to Allied harmony and the limited agreement reached at Potsdam. The Soviets argued that, as capitalism had brought about the rise of Adolf Hitler, then de-nazification and re-education required the nationalization of the means of production in the Soviet zone. Walter Ulbricht, a leading German Communist who had fled to Moscow in 1933, was flown back to Berlin in May 1945, and began to organize the political system in the Soviet zone. By May 1946 the Communist and Social Democratic Parties in the Soviet zone were merged into the Socialist Unity Party, with Communist dogma and leadership very much to the fore.

With the Western Allies resisting any reparations from current production in Germany, relations between East and West became all the more sour. The Soviet zone was stripped, often in inefficient haste, of much of its capital equipment, which was then sent east, often just to rust away in railway sidings. The Soviets took up their claims, as agreed at Potsdam, on the

German economy in the Western zones, but frequently reneged on the agreement to send in return food and raw materials to the West from the Soviet zone. Without question the Soviet Union and many of the areas under its control were in dire economic straits, and there were areas of famine inside the Soviet Union itself. But at the time most Western policy makers took a very dim view of Soviet behaviour over the reparations deal, such as it was. Stubborn Soviet insistence on repeatedly raising the reparations question at the foreign ministers' meetings which regularly followed Potsdam, as agreed at Yalta, and forceful attempts to regularize the reparations from all of Germany even more in Moscow's favour, came to be interpreted not only as a device for ameliorating the Soviet Union's plight – especially as the United States would not extend lend-lease or give a requested loan – but as an attempt to undermine the economic and political recovery of Europe for Soviet political ends.[21] As the increasing cost of sustaining the fabric of society in occupied Germany came to be felt by the Western powers, particularly Britain, Soviet behaviour over reparations came to be viewed in a hostile light and greatly contributed to an adversarial environment.

In an effort to reduce the costs of sustaining their German zones, the Western powers raised the permitted level of industrial output in 1946, and Britain and the United States began serious consideration of a merging of their zones into one economic unit. In reality this meant the United States relieving a struggling Britain of much of the cost of maintaining its zone, estimated at £80 million for 1946–47. In January 1947 the British and American zones fused into one unit of economic administration, against a background of Anglo-American frustration over Soviet reluctance to administer Germany as one economic unit, as agreed at Potsdam. Meanwhile, in the time between Potsdam and 'Bizonia', the political developments outside Germany had failed to contribute to any strengthening of trust between East and West in Germany itself. The dropping of the atomic bombs on Hiroshima and Nagasaki in August 1945 debarred the Soviets from any major military contribution to the war in the Far East and from any major role in the political settlement there.

The Second World War ended with the introduction of the atomic age, and a new and awe-inspiring dimension was

introduced into East–West competition. The Soviet Union
resisted the Baruch Plan proposals to internationalize atomic
power, and set about pursuing its own atomic weapons
programme as quickly as it could. In March 1946 Churchill
made his famous 'Iron Curtain' speech' at Fulton, Missouri,
painting a miserable picture of an ideologically divided Europe
with the Soviet Union and the Western Allies as the protagonists.
In February 1947 the British government requested United
States aid in warding off Communist insurgency in Greece and
Moscow's pressure on Turkey. The result was a major United
States military involvement in the Eastern Mediterranean, and a
clear ideological message from President Truman in March 1947
– the Truman Doctrine – pledging the United States' support for
democracy wherever threatened. Throughout East Europe in
1947 and 1948 the ascendancy of the Communist Party was
established in areas liberated by the Red Army, and any
instances of pluralistic government were diluted to insignificance
or removed altogether. Particularly alarming to the West was the
case of Czechoslovakia:

> The growing political uniformity of the East European
> regimes was dramatically underscored in February 1948
> with the Communist coup in Czechoslovakia. The resigna-
> tion of twelve non-communist ministers from the coalition
> government that month led to the demand, backed up by
> intense Soviet diplomatic pressure combined with veiled
> threats of armed interference, for the formation of a new
> government more overtly under communist control. Sens-
> ing his country's isolation, President Edward Benes com-
> plied with the demands, and the last vestige of popular
> accountability disappeared from the East European poli-
> tical landscape.[22]

In the West every effort was being made to support
democratic–capitalist governments in France and Italy, particularly with Marshall Aid funds sustaining the economies. The
Czechoslovakian episode of 1948 supplied the final encouragement for the formation of a defence coalition of West European
states – a notion the British had been sponsoring since 1947. The
Brussels Treaty of March 1948, which brought Britain, France

and the Benelux countries into military alliance, was very much an attempt by London to entangle the United States in a formal European defence commitment. In this it was successful. The example of the Brussels Treaty, and of West Europeans attempting to help themselves, persuaded Congress and the executive in Washington to agree to the North Atlantic Alliance, which was to come into being in April 1949. Throughout 1948 in the Western zones of Germany plans were under way for the unification of all three zones and for major currency reform in an effort to enhance economic recovery along democratic–capitalist lines. The introduction of the new currency in June 1948 throughout the Western zones, including West Berlin, and the subsequent walk out by the Soviets from the Allied Control Council put an end to the pretence that Germany was being run as one economic unit. A *de facto* partition of defeated Germany was under way, and in its train the ideological division of Europe.

In response to the West's currency reforms and the gradual evolution of a West German state, the Soviet Union launched a blockade of West Berlin, over 100 kilometres inside the Soviet zone. All overland routes were blocked, and electrical power cut off. The expulsion of the Western Allies from West Berlin would have undermined Western prestige and left the rest of West Europe unsure of Anglo-American commitment or future intentions. The prudent use of the airlift spun out the crisis and averted open war, but in Western eyes the blockade confirmed malevolent Soviet intentions, and the North Atlantic Treaty was signed in Washington in April 1949, formally committing the United States to West European defence. In practical terms a very important step had already been taken, one month into the blockade.

In July 1948 the National Security Council in Washington ordered the dispatch of sixty B-29s – 'atomic bombers' – to Britain. Atomic weapons were now introduced into the European theatre, and the deterrent threat was being explicitly utilized as an instrument of policy. In the month following the signing of the North Atlantic Treaty the Berlin blockade was abandoned, and the state of the Federal Republic of Germany (FRG) was founded; by October the German Democratic Republic (GDR)

had been created in the Soviet zone. In 1949 both the Soviet
Union and the Western Allies supported the goal of a single
Germany, but one not ideologically at odds with either Moscow's
or Washington's view of the world. A united Germany would be
too powerful economically and too important strategically to be
allowed to fall under the control of the other side, but the
ideological disparity between the West and the East made
agreement over economic and political objectives impossible.
Where blame should be placed is now immaterial. It is not
impossible to find fault with the behaviour of both sides, but
given their objectives, based upon preconceived ideological
perspectives, it is hardly surprising that the cautious and
suspicious cooperation of 1941–45 should by 1949 have turned to
bitter competition over the spoils of war:

> Between 1939 and 1945 the United Nations, whose
> common hostility to Germany formed the only bond that
> held them together, were divided into two groups – the
> Soviet Union on one side and bourgeois democracies on the
> other – which were bound to oppose each other when the
> Third Reich floundered. Rarely can hostility have been so
> predictable. The Germans never ceased to proclaim the
> fact, and Goebbels was unable to understand that the more
> he insisted the more he forced the Americans to camouflage
> it. Not for a moment, of course, did the Russian authorities
> forget; but the Anglo Saxons, and particularly the Amer-
> icans, often acted as if they did not regard the hostility as
> fundamental.[23]

In the West policy makers and the public at large were ill at
ease with such ideological rivalry and hostility in the early
postwar period. Only a few years before the Czechoslovakian *coup
d'état*, the Berlin blockade, the establishment of the Federal
Republic of Germany and the creation of the North Atlantic
Alliance, the Soviet Union had been a wartime ally of the
Western powers, and its qualities had been eulogized by Western
governmental propaganda machines. In more recent years the
peoples of East and West have become used to the ideological
nature of East–West competition but, none the less, in historical
terms, in peace or in war, it is a unique state of international

relations. Such prolonged and intense ideological rivalry as that of the past forty years has not been seen in Europe since the era of the French revolutionary wars and Napoleon Bonaparte. Between 1792 and 1815 war and revolution were 'inextricably mixed',[24] and the *ancien régime* of feudalism and absolutism came under an immense challenge from liberal and egalitarian notions during the Enlightenment. Certainly, the Second World War came to be portrayed, amongst other things, as a war of ideas – decency versus Fascism and Nazism (indecency). For the Russians, it was very much a war between nation-states – the Great Patriotic War – and the ideological implications were deliberately underplayed, particularly when times were especially tough for the Soviet Union. Stalin had little doubt that the Russian people would bear considerable hardship for the sake of Mother Russia, but not for the creed of Marxism–Leninism. Likewise in the West, in the popular mind it was Germany, the old enemy, rather than just a political creed, that was once again a threat. Indeed, the Western democracies went to war in 1939 primarily for traditional reasons of balance of power and state security: 'Britain declared war in September 1939 more for traditional reasons than in the spirit of a crusade against Nazism; indeed it is conceivable that had Hitler been willing to withdraw from Poland and discuss terms in a reasonable way Chamberlain and Halifax would have been willing to negotiate.'[25] Only in the later years of the war, with the policy of unconditional surrender and with the demands put upon the civilian population by total war, did the annihilation of the ideas and social practices of Hitlerian Germany assume in the West any prominence in the catalogue of war objectives.

In 1914 the competing alliance systems had not been at odds ideologically:

> The condition of the alliances in 1914 placed the western parliamentary democracies of France and Great Britain in the same camp as autocratic Russia, just as it made ill-assorted allies of the German national Reich with its ultramodern economy and efficient military organisation, and ramshackle, multi-national, antiquated Austria–Hungary, and before long Turkey of the Young Turks.

None of the powers in 1914 was more than a semi-democratic state in that none rested on truly universal suffrage. But since the presence or absence of democratic institutions was not one of the differentials between the belligerents, democratic ideals were not a war aim in 1914. The only war aims were self-defence and victory.[26]

The notion that the war was being fought for high ideals did not come to bear until the collapse of Russia and the Russian Revolution in 1917, when the awful costs of the conflict required vindication by some purpose other than grand strategy. The entry of the United States into the war in 1917, in the guise of the New World coming to save the corrupt Old World encouraged the notion that the war was being fought for higher ideals than were in fact the objectives of 1914 and 1915:

To win sympathy in the world, and maintain the morale of their suffering nations, governments resorted to ideology, and that element played an important part in the allied conduct in the war from the time of the American intervention and the Russian Revolution. The war had not been started in order to bring about the triumph of particular views of life and society; but as the cost of operations mounted these views were felt to be essential to inflate the prospective profits of victory. It was declared that the peace would be durable only if it were dictated unconditionally after crushing the enemy. The demand for total victory was not so much the expression of a political philosophy as a reflex reaction to total war.[27]

When in August 1914 three wars broke out, strategic considerations turned these local conflicts into a world war. The three wars involved Austria against Serbia, Germany and Austria versus Russia and France, and Britain against Imperial Germany. Military necessity, strategic planning, and alliance relationships formal and informal, linked the three sets of hostilities together.[28] The primary consideration of the Entente powers was to control the burgeoning might of Germany and sustain a balance of power in Europe:

From the moment there was formed in the centre of Europe

a German Empire, industrially foremost in Europe, with a population exceeding France by more than 50 per cent, and allied to the dual monarchy, a war on the small scale of that of 1870 had become impossible. Neither Russia nor Great Britain would have tolerated a new German victory which would have made the Reich no longer merely the dominant European state, but a claimant to empire over the Continent.[29]

The tension which produced this war was derived not from philosophical differences, but from political–strategic competition between Austria and Russia in the Balkans, imperial competition between France and Germany in Morocco, the Anglo-German naval arms race, and the land arms race between all the continental powers.

Similarly, in the nineteenth century, the limited and localized wars which had occurred were dynastic, preserving local balances of power or attempting to sustain crumbling imperial frontiers. None of the thirteen separate wars waged in Europe (not counting conflicts involving European states outside Europe) between 1815 and 1914 had led to a general European war, because the general European balance of power had not been threatened. The results of the Crimean War, the Austro-Prussian War of 1866 or the Franco-Prussian War of 1870, for instance, had not seriously endangered the security of the non-belligerent powers in Europe. The predominant philosophy of post-Napoleonic nineteenth-century Europe was nationalism, but although nationalist aspirations certainly formed the basis of many of the wars of this period, nineteenth century European nationalism hardly constituted an ideology. None of the wars of the post-Napoleonic period threatened or changed the economic or social establishments of the belligerent powers, despite severe loss of territory or prestige, as in the case of France in 1870. Indeed, in France in 1871, when the Paris Commune attempted to create a new social order and implement ideological change, the revolutionaries were crushed by French military power. The new nation-states of nineteenth century Europe, born out of nationalism and war, were deeply conformist in their political, economic and social organization.

The introduction of ideology into conflict arouses passions and anxieties. While populations may be reconciled to defeat if the result is to be the loss of overseas or even national territories, or the denial of access to certain markets or sources of raw materials, or the payment over a few years of manageable reparations, the prospect of drastic social and economic change in their daily lives is not easily accommodated. In the years since the end of the Second World War there have been limited extra European wars, with one of the superpowers directly or closely involved: for instance, the Korean War of 1950–53, the major United States military involvement in south-east Asia in 1964–73, and the Angolan civil war of 1975. In these instances and many others, though not in all cases of limited war since 1945, ideology has been the fundamental consideration determining the alignment of the rival camps. For instance, if the Moscow-oriented Movimento Popular de Libertação in Angola (MPLA) had not been Marxist, then one strongly suspects that they would not have sought, or received, aid from Moscow and direct military assistance from Havana. One doubts if the United States would have become entrapped in south-east Asia in the 1960s if there had been a non-Marxist authoritarian regime in Hanoi seeking the historic objective of Vietnamese unification and hegemony in the region. Nevertheless, notwithstanding the prevalence and pervasiveness of ideological rivalry in the international system over the past forty years, which quickly developed into a near-duopolistic United States–Soviet affair, there has been no direct US–Soviet military conflict, nor in Europe a NATO–WP military conflict. Great care seems to have been taken by the respective superpowers to construct concepts of foreign policy behaviour which legitimize ideological competition, but simultaneously control and manage that competition within the bounds of acceptable costs. Ideological conflict has been controlled, deliberately, by the political concepts and diplomatic processes of containment, peaceful coexistence, and *détente*, the common characteristics of which are the sustenance by the rival blocs of a predetermined ideological position but the avoidance, by a variety of means, of open war.

Containment

On 2 September 1945 the Japanese Empire surrendered and the Second World War came to an end. The objective of the United States government of President Truman, as with his predecessor Franklin Roosevelt, was a return to 'normalcy' as quickly as possible. The Truman administration was well aware of the unfinished political business between the Allies in Europe and the difficult obstacles to be surmounted, but there was a feeling amongst many in government that tough political bargaining could produce an acceptable resolution. At this time there was a reluctance in Washington to come to grips with the ideological nature of the Soviet Union and appreciate the perspective of the Soviet leaders in Moscow. Between May 1945 when the war came to an end in Europe, and March 1946, the United States Army was reduced from 3.5 million in uniform to 400,000. In the few months following victory there was a blindness to the immutable differences between East and West, despite the difficulties experienced at Potsdam and the early problems of four-power management in Germany. However, eighteen months after the end of hostilities, on 12 March 1947, President Truman addressed a joint session of Congress in these terms:

> I believe that it must be the policy of the United States to support free peoples who are resisting attempted subjugation by armed minorities or by outside pressures. I believe that we must assist free peoples to work out their own destinies in their own way. I believe that our help should be primarily through economic and financial aid which is essential to economic stability and orderly political progress . . .
> Our way of life is based on the will of the majority, and is distinguished by free institutions, representative government, free elections . . . The second way of life is based upon the will of the minority forcibly imposed upon the majority. It relies upon terror and oppression . . . The free peoples of the world look to us for support in maintaining their freedom . . . If we falter in our leadership, we may

endanger the peace of the world – and we shall surely
endanger the welfare of our nation.[30]

What became known as the Truman Doctrine – an apparent
commitment to the role of democracy's global policeman – arose
from a direct appeal by London to Washington for aid in
carrying out traditional duties in the Eastern Mediterranean.
Greece was again in the midst of bitter civil war, with the
prospect of the Communist rebels gaining the ascendancy, and
Turkey was being put under political pressure by Soviet
demands to share control of the sea route from the Aegean into
the Black Sea. In the grip of struggles to revive its economy,
severely weakened by six years of war effort, Britain could not
spare the vital resources to economically prop up the Greek
government, nor deploy adequate military power as a deterrent
to Soviet designs on Turkey. Throughout the winter of 1946–47
thoughts in Washington had been turning towards how to
manage an intractable Soviet Union with apparent hostile and
expansionist tendencies. Truman had taken the opportunity to
translate a specific request for aid for a particular purpose into a
grand, enunciation of purpose for United States foreign policy.
In his statement he had recognized the ideological nature of the
contest, and prescribed a foreign policy to deal with it. On 12
March 1947, 'policy began to catch up with ideology.'[31]

Truman deliberately designed his speech to catch the public's
attention and to garner support for a foreign policy that was
turning its back on 'normalcy' and the American tradition of
non-entanglement in international affairs outside the Americas,
lauding the United States' duty to protect the ideals upon which
American society is based and has prospered. While many of the
foreign affairs experts, though suspicious of Soviet intentions,
were alarmed at the scope of Truman's pledge and anxious about
the capabilities of the United States to fulfil such commitments,
they did not appreciate the domestic context: 'Truman was the
expert on domestic politics . . . Truman realised that he could
never get the economy-minded Republicans – and the public that
stood behind them – to shell out tax dollars to support a rather
shabby king in Greece. Truman had to describe the Greek
situation in universal terms, good versus evil, to get support for

containment.'[32] What was happening in the Eastern Mediterranean was important to Western security interests, psychologically if not in practice. At the time the perception in London and in Washington was that the fall of Greece and then perhaps Turkey to Communist subversion and pressure would have a domino effect throughout the Middle East. But the Truman Doctrine set the tone for Western, especially United States, perceptions of Soviet intentions for the next twenty years, with only a few lulls, throughout the international system – not just in the Eastern Mediterranean or in central Europe, which was the focus for concern in the late 1940s. The irony is that the main instigator of the Greek civil war was not Stalin, but Tito of Yugoslavia, with acquisitive designs on Macedonia. Tito demonstrated the brittle nature of Soviet control and the constraints on the reach of Soviet military and political power by breaking away from Stalin's camp in 1948.

Undoubtedly, by 1947 the United States' government was fearful of Soviet expansion into West Europe, which would pose the prospect of upsetting the balance of power. But, the real fear was very much that of political expansion, rather than military conquest. United States foreign policy was to contain Soviet influence where it was, primarily by political and economic means. Economic and military aid were dispatched to the Eastern Mediterranean in 1947, and Greece and Turkey did not fall into the Communist orbit. But the foremost manifestation of the Truman notion of sustaining democracy where it existed, and the major instrument of what was being called 'containment', was the Marshall Plan – the 17 billion dollars worth of United States economic aid given to West Europe – one of the few stipulations being that the European recipients jointly administer the aid through the Organization for European Economic Cooperation (OEEC), a condition which prevented Stalin from allowing East European participation.[33]

In the month preceding the Truman speech an anti-Communist consensus was emerging within the administration, and the Truman speech was an expression of mounting anxiety and the search for a strategy. 'In other words, the doctrine was not a cynical manoeuvre, as some writers have since argued.'[34] By repute, the intellectual driving force behind the containment doctrine was a senior state department official and a Soviet expert, George Kennan. The July 1947 issue of the prestigious international affairs journal, *Foreign Affairs*, published an article entitled 'The Sources of Soviet Conduct', under the anonymous authorship of 'X'. George Kennan was the author, a fact that was soon made public. Seen to be of such importance that it was excerpted in *Life* and *Reader's Digest* magazines and discussed throughout the national press, the 'X article' did much to create a popular image of United States foreign policy towards the Soviet Union. Kennan wrote that the hostility of the Soviet Union 'Will be with us, whether in the foreground or the background, until the internal nature of Soviet power is changed . . . In these circumstances it is clear that the main element of any United States policy towards the Soviet Union must be that of a long-term, patient but firm and vigilant containment of Russian expansive tendencies.'[35] Kennan seemed to be aruguing for a global response, of a military nature, to Soviet global expansionist probes wherever they might occur: 'the adroit and vigilant application of counter-force at a series of constantly shifting geographical and political points corresponding to the shifts and manoeuvres of Soviet policy.'[36]

Kennan did not in fact think the the Soviets posed a military threat. As is clear from his writings and lectures of this period, some of which predate the publication of the 'X article', he believed that the United States' response to Soviet foreign policy should be selective and primarily non-military, as the Soviet threat was itself primarily non-military.[37] He admits in his *Memoirs* that the 'X article' was poorly drafted and could easily be understood to mean the opposite of what he intended.[38] None the less, it soon came to be accepted as 'the quasi-official statement of American foreign policy'.[39] It was now that the term 'containment', used by Kennan, came into the language of United States foreign policy, and what he wrote in the 'X article' seemed to square with the Truman speech of March 1947. Indeed, it was assumed that Kennan had had a major influence on it while in reality he was horrified by the universal commitment that the Truman speech implied.[40] Kennan did have considerable influence on United States foreign policy at this time. In February 1946, while at the Moscow Embassy, he had despatched an 8,000-word telegram on Soviet behaviour and intentions which, by all accounts, had had a major effect on policy makers in Washington, opening their eyes to the nature of the Soviet regime and the reality of the problems facing Washington in its relations with Moscow.[41] That telegram had done what George Kennan intended it to do. Indeed, he had been surprised by its effect. The 'X article' misfired, but it is remembered to this day, and it influenced the conduct of United States foreign policy for over twenty years: 'To Kennan's regret, its ideas were used for years and decades to justify Cold War policies which he himself, then and later, found excessively militaristic, ideological, and universalistic.'[42]

However, whatever the confusion or misunderstanding over the scope or the instruments of containment, what was clear was that the United States had no intention of using the atomic bomb or waging conventional war, or of deploying political or economic instruments, to expel Soviet influence and control from the Soviet zone in Germany, from Poland, from Hungary, or wherever else the Red Army stopped in Europe in 1945. Containment meant keeping Soviet influence and power where it was, not rolling it back to its 1939 or 1941 borders. The irony of the 'X article' is that while it seemed to propose an all-embracing containment strategy, which in fact its author did not support, subsequent events in East–West relations appeared to vindicate both the Truman Doctrine and the 'X article': 'Buttressed by the success of containment in Greece (which in fact owed much to the Stalin–Tito split) the Kennan article became the gospel of American foreign policy.'[43]

In October 1947 it was revealed in a *Pravda* article that delegates meeting in Poland from nine European Communist parties, including France and Italy, had established a Communist Information Bureau (Cominform). This was a successor to the Comintern, disbanded as a mark of Allied solidarity by Stalin in 1943. It was made clear that the Cominform's purpose was to lead the ideological struggle into the non-Soviet world. The world was divided into two camps: the imperialist camp led by the United States, and the peace-loving Communist camp. The Soviet Union was acknowledged by Cominform as legitimate leader of the peace-loving camp. In February 1948 the shaky coalition government of Czechoslovakia, in which the Communist Party played the major role, caved in to Communist demands and pressures. Czechoslovakia, from being a kind of no man's land between Soviet-controlled East Europe and democratic–capitalist West Europe, was pulled into the Soviet orbit. Following the Czechoslovakian coup, the United States began to rearm, and President Truman expressed public interest in a Western military alliance on the day in March 1948 that the Brussels Pact was signed in Europe. To entangle the United States in West European defence was a major objective of the Europeans, not least the British, but West Europe had to demonstrate to Congress that it was trying to help itself. The Brussels Pact fulfilled that requirement. The Berlin blockade of 1948/49 and the breakdown of any pretence of four power control in Germany and in its capital city appeared to be the ultimate vindication for the strategy of containment in Europe. Europe came the nearest to war it had been since the surrender of Nazi Germany in 1945. Maximum western resolve and steadfastness were required in the face of a Soviet attempt to change the 1945 status quo and undermine the basis of any confidence the continental West Europeans, especially the West Germans, might have had in the Anglo-American commitment.

However, while events in Europe may have been justifying the anxieties expressed by Truman and Kennan, it was events in the Far East which transformed containment from a European strategy, primarily political, into a global and military strategy, as the interested public thought Truman and Kennan intended it to be. In 1949 the civil war in China came to a conclusion with the expulsion of the Nationalist forces to the island of Formosa, and the occupation of all of mainland China by the successful Communist forces of Mao Tse Tung. In June 1950, against the backdrop of the successful testing of a Soviet atomic bomb a few months earlier in November 1949, the North Koreans' Communist regime attacked non-Communist South Korea with a full-blooded military assault. It was assumed that Moscow, probing for weak spots in the external world, was directing the North Korean attack. A considerable United States military force, with some other Western contingents, under UN auspices, eventually turned the military tide. A mistake was made in the attempt to liberate North Korea, which in turn led to the introduction of Chinese 'volunteers' into the conflict. To control the war and limit its scope Truman was obliged to dismiss General MacArthur and settle for less than total victory, yet at considerable cost.

The lessons of Korea for the United States seemed to be that containment required a strong military instrument, but that military force had to be used sparingly – otherwise open superpower conflict was the prospect. After Korea a large United States defence establishment in peacetime became the norm, and containment became a global, military strategy. In 1951 a permanent NATO military bureaucracy was established in Paris, and General Eisenhower was appointed first Supreme Allied Commander Europe, in charge of an integrated defence force for Europe. Initially Washington had viewed the North Atlantic Treaty as a traditional military guarantee pact, where a major United States commitment could be called upon only when required. The Korean War and the subsequent decision to organize permanent standing forces for NATO use changed all that. From 1951 'the United States became a *fixed* part of the continental balance of power.'[44] But there was universal agreement amongst all members of NATO that the alliance was defensive, not redistributive. Aggression would need to be committed against one of the members in the North Atlantic area defined by the treaty for the alliance to be activated, and then only in pursuit of status quo objectives. The containment line established in Europe was soon extended to the Middle and Far East, as the globalization and militarization of the doctrine continued apace. In 1954 the United States was the patron power behind the establishment of the South East Asian Treaty Organization (SEATO), which also included Britain, France, Australia, New Zealand, the Philippines, Pakistan and Thailand. A protocol extended SEATO to include Vietnam, Laos and Cambodia. In 1955 the United States encouraged the Baghdad Pact – a military alliance composed of Britain, Turkey, Iran, Iraq and Pakistan.

In the twenty years following the Korean War a variety of military strategies were used to underpin containment in all the alliances strung around the periphery of the Communist world, including Europe. For most of the 1950s the strategy was massive retaliation – the notion that Communist advances could be prevented by the deterrent threat of a massive response by United States nuclear military power. While the American homeland remained relatively invulnerable to Soviet nuclear reprisal, massive retaliation was deemed to be credible, but with the Soviet acquisition of ICBM capability in the late 1950s it was seen to be no longer a credible response to all contingencies.

The incoming administration of President Kennedy in 1961 adopted a military strategy of flexible response, at conventional and nuclear level. To avoid the dilemma of a total response or no response at all, the United States would strive for as many options as possible with which to respond to any kind of Communist aggression. It soon found itself obliged to prepare for limited wars, and indeed confronted one in south–east Asia. In pursuit of containment the US committed 500,000 troops to the defence of South Vietnam in the 1960s, and suffered over 50,000 casualties. Yet, while there were long-range United States air strikes to North Vietnam in efforts to cripple the aggressor's war effort and break supply lines to the guerrilla forces in the south, there was never any real prospect of a United States or South Vietnamese invasion of the north and the roll-back of the Communist threat to the Sino-Vietnamese border. Containment was meant to control and limit the ideological conflict, not escalate it.

In the 1952 presidential election campaign the rhetoric of 'roll-back' and 'liberation' was used by the successful Republican Party when discussing United States–Soviet relations, and the focus of such language was Europe. But in office, caution and prudence prevailed. Eisenhower was not a president to take unwarranted risks, and in that he was supported by his West European allies. In June 1953 there were riots in Berlin and other East German cities which the Red Army crushed. There were riots in Poland in 1956 which led to a limited degree of change in the organization of the Polish economy and to some trappings of political autonomy: for instance, the Soviet troops stationed in Poland were linked to the Warsaw Pact arrangements, rather than remaining there in a state of military occupation. But the threat of Soviet military involvement perpetuated Polish deference to Moscow's wishes. The most tragic case of the oppression of a libertarian movement in East Europe in the 1950s was in Hungary in October and November 1956. In Poland, the unrest was within the Communist Party; in Hungary it was against the Communist Party. Events in Poland encouraged a popular uprising in Hungary against a corrupt and incompetent Communist regime. Fighting began on 23 October between Soviet forces in Hungary and revolutionary committees, workers' councils, student groups and others who wished to see political reform. On 27 October a new government was formed including some prominent non-Communists. On 28 October a cease-fire was announced, and on the 30 and 31st Soviet forces withdrew from Budapest. Nagy, the new Communist premier, announced that Hungary would become a multi-party state, leave the Warsaw Pact, and become neutral. On 1 November Soviet reinforcements poured into Hungary and on the 4th a number of major cities were attacked with vigour and overpowering military force. Courageous resistance by a few Hungarian army units and many civilians was of no avail. Fighting continued for some time but the Red Army was soon in control, and Janos Kadar, a former member of the Nagy government, was persuaded to assume the reigns of power. Hungary was to remain a single-party Communist state within the Warsaw Pact. In the winter of 1956–57 nearly 200,000 refugees escaped across the Austrian frontier to the West.[45]

Throughout all these East European crises, in 1953 and 1956, the United States chose to sit on the sidelines:

> Liberation was the Republican party's therapy for a public that refused to accept the facts of America's limited power in the world and rejected any changes in its traditional approach to foreign policy. That this policy of liberation was probably never meant to be more than a verbal appeal to the American people was clearly demonstrated by the anti-communist revolt in East Berlin and other East German cities in June 1953 and during the national uprising in Hungary in late 1956. In neither case did the Eisenhower administration act – except to condemn the Soviet Union for its oppression of Germans and Hungarians and to express sympathy for the victims of Soviet despotism. In Berlin, it substituted food packages to the

East Berliners for liberation; and in Hungary, it even reassured the Soviet Union that it had no intention of intervening. The status quo was thereby reaffirmed. Liberation had returned to the womb of containment.[46]

The other Western states, even if they had felt motivated and inclined to intervene in support of the Nagy government in Hungary in November 1956, could not do so without the United States' lead and support. Indeed, Britain and France, the two other major Western powers, were at the exact time of the Hungarian uprising deeply embroiled in military intervention in the Middle East, and in disagreement with the United States over their management of the Suez crisis. In practice, the actions of the Soviets in disciplining the Hungarians, and the actions of the United States in constraining its allies in the Middle East painted a picture of a distinctly bipolar world where the two ideological rivals kept their own camps in order, while respecting the rights of the other in their own spheres of influence. Likewise in 1968, when the Soviet Union and some of its Warsaw Pact allies invaded Czechoslovakia in order to remove the liberalizing Dubcek administration, the United States did little but postpone talks on stategic arms limitation, and then only briefly.

Nevertheless, in the world outside the Soviet bloc, containment demanded the use of military force to keep from the Communists what did not belong to them already. The lines of demarcation in Europe appeared firm and distinct, but the decolonizing Third World, to which Khrushchev in 1956 and 1961 made public declarations of support for 'wars of national liberation', appeared to successive governments in Washington to be a primary area of concern. In the 1950s and 1960s there was a perception of a monolithic Communist bloc with Moscow at its heart encouraging insurgency wherever the opportunity arose. In 1960 the United States looked upon itself as having the role of containing the perceived Communist conspiracy. President Kennedy in 1962 stated that 'for the next ten or twenty years the burden will be placed completely on our country for the preservation of freedom.'[47] President Johnson, in 1965, declared 'History and our own achievements have thrust upon us the principal responsibility for the protection of freedom on earth.'[48]

Containment held fast in Europe, but came under severe pressure in south–east Asia. The costs of the war in Vietnam – political as well as economic and military – produced a reassessment of containment as a universalist military doctrine. The United States could not afford, politically or economically, to be the global policeman of John Kennedy's and Lyndon Johnson's imagery. Each perceived challenge to Western interests would have to be assessed in its own right, and it could not be assumed that the United States would always take up the burden. It was fortuitous that the international environment was conducive to changes in the late 1960s. While throughout most of the 1950s it was correct to identify a monolithic Moscow-centred Communist bloc, by 1970 this was patently not the case. The Sino-Soviet split was clear for all to see, and it was erroneous to assume that any challenge which could be labelled either Marxist or Communist was under the tight control of Moscow, or would be so for long.

Up to 1969 military planners in Washington planned, on paper, for a '$2\frac{1}{2}$' war strategy:

1 a ninety-day defence of West Europe against the Soviet Union;
2 a sustained defence against attack by the People's Republic of China on South Korea or south-east Asia;
3 a more limited contingency elsewhere – for example, the Middle East.

In 1969 Richard Nixon came to office as president, and with him Henry Kissinger as his assistant for national security affairs. In October 1969 Kissinger advised Nixon on the desirability of a change from a '$2\frac{1}{2}$' war strategy to a '$1\frac{1}{2}$' war strategy. In Kissinger's mind, the prospect of a joint Sino-Soviet move against the United States had become most unlikely. Even if it was likely, the impression should not be given that it would be met with conventional forces. Nixon's enunciation of the '$1\frac{1}{2}$' war strategy in his foreign policy report to Congress on 18 February 1970 clearly signalled that the Red Chinese threat in Asia was being downgraded, but that the Soviet Union was still viewed as the major threat, and the locale of that threat was Europe. In effect, containment was being 'de-universalized' and regionalized. In Asia, nations threatened by insurgencies and civil war would be required first of all to help themselves, especially in the area of ground forces, though some economic aid would be forthcoming, depending upon the circumstances. The United States would still stick by its treaty commitments in Asia, but the automatic involvement of large ground forces in any challenge to the status quo implied by the rhetoric of successive presidents from Truman to Kennedy was not to be expected.

The Nixon Doctrine (sometimes known as the Guam Doctrine, as he made his initial remarks about the changes in Guam in July 1969 en route to the Philippines) signalled the end of containment as understood for the previous twenty years and more.[49] For Europe, however, regional containment continued: here the lines of political demarcation were clear, and infringements would not be tolerated. However, the international political environment in which the defence of the democracies of West Europe was being sustained was changing.

Peaceful coexistence

For the past thirty years the ideological doctrine of peaceful coexistence has guided Soviet foreign policy in its relations with the international system, and particularly with the West. Contrary to the image projected by the phrase, peaceful coexistence does not eschew ideological conflict, but endorses the continuing struggle across the East–West divide. In this regard continuity has been maintained in Soviet foreign policy. Prior to the peaceful coexistence of the post Stalin leadership, the dominant foreign policy concept was that of two camps – the Soviet camp and the non-Communist camp, between which there was inevitable struggle and from which the Soviet-led camp would emerge victorious. This theory subscribed to the Marxist–Leninist 'inevitability of war' thesis which foresaw massive armed struggle, albeit initially between capitalist states, between the Communist camp and the bourgeoisie, regardless of international circumstances. The two-camps doctrine was dominant in the latter years of Stalin's rule, and both sustained and reflected the regime's 'laager' mentality and fears of capitalist encirclement.

The notion of coexistence with the hostile non-Communist world was not novel to the Soviet Union in the 1950s. With the death of Stalin and the consolidation of the Western bloc in West Europe, manifested in particular by the prospective rearming of West Germany, it was evident that the bellicose two-camps doctrine was not yielding dividends. Soviet ambitions for a European security arrangement acceptable to Moscow appeared less likely at the time of Stalin's death than at any time since 1945. Plans for some kind of *modus vivendi* with the West surfaced amongst Stalin's early successors, Malenkov and Bulganin, and there were precedents to which they could point. In the period 1921–23, when the Soviet Union was struggling to establish itself as a Communist state in a hostile world, both Lenin and Stalin had pursued the normalization of relations and increased trade with capitalist countries in an effort to build up a Communist base. Lenin called this 'peaceful cohabitation', and recognized it as a short term expedient.[50] Naturally, this was a pragmatic policy, and revolutionary opportunities abroad, given low costs, were to be pursued. At this early stage in the evolution of the Soviet state, doctrine was not deemed to be inflexible, though ultimate ideological objectives were held to be sacrosanct.

The central theme of the continuing ideological struggle was sustained in the post-Stalin years, even while a coexistence relationship was being sought. Indeed, there are even indications that Stalin was contemplating reducing tensions with the West, if for no other reasons than to provide a respite in East–West animosity in order to allow a consolidation of Soviet control in East Europe.[51]

In the intra-party struggle following Stalin's death in 1953, Malenkov, his immediate successor, attempted to pursue a temporary peaceful co-existence policy, for the purpose of permitting the Soviet Union to concentrate its national energies on economic recovery and rising living standards. An important aspect of this initiative was the introduction of the concept of deterrence into Soviet political–strategic thinking by Malenkov and Mikoyan in March 1954.[52] Given the nature of modern weaponry, Malenkov argued, an East–West conflict could lead to the destruction of the world rather than the triumph of Communism. The policy of fighting wars rather than deterring them was seen to be very costly, while an emphasis on a nuclear minimum deterrent rather than a continual conventional arms build-up would release resources which could be devoted to the Soviet economy. However, in the period 1953–55 there was an opposing coalition within the Soviet leadership, led by Khrushchev and Bulganin and with the apparent support of the military. The coalition adopted a traditionalist view and opposed the peaceful coexistence policies of Malenkov. This was not only for internal political reasons within the CPSU, but because the coalition held that it takes two to constitute a deterrence scenario.[53] Given the apparent hostility and rhetoric of the Eisenhower/Dulles foreign policy posture, and the decision of the NATO Council in 1954 to use nuclear weapons in any future European war, many of the Soviet leaders were uncertain about Western intentions. Would NATO truly only use nuclear weapons for defence, thereby being forced to detonate them, for instance, on West German soil?

Malenkov was dispossessed of the premiership in February 1955, but the build-up of forces which could be used for the purposes of deterrence continued, the argument being that long-range bombers also constituted a directly offensive weapon. Indeed, the creation of uncertainty in the minds of Western decision-makers had, and always will have, a useful political function. The ability of the Soviet Union to invoke for self-serving political purposes the image or even prospect of a global nuclear war provided the Soviet decision-makers with a powerful new instrument of foreign policy. Such a potential was attributed to the Soviets by the West because of the perceived 'bomber gap' which existed in the mid 1950s. Through the skilful use of the Aviation Day military parade in 1955, the Soviets led Western observers to believe that they possessed a huge long-range bomber force. The Soviet Union, it was hoped, would now be seen to be a global power. However, in the year following Malenkov's fall from authority, Khrushchev, now the major political power in the Soviet Union, must have modified his views on the military and foreign policy of the Soviet Union. The Geneva summit of July 1955 almost certainly marked a turning-point in his strategic thinking: he appears to have become convinced that the West was committed to defensive containment. Now, with Khrushchev's estimate of the threat posed to Soviet security by superior United States strategic forces drastically reduced, a crude concept of deterrence began to occupy a new high place in Soviet military thought, and against this background of security a new and more permanent doctrine of peaceful coexistence was introduced at the CPSU 20th Congress in February 1956. At this momentous gathering, where Khrushchev launched his attack on Stalinism, he enunciated a new ideological base for Soviet foreign policy which constituted, in many ways, a distinct break with the past. Just as the Western doctrine of containment was an exercise in realism, Khrushchev's peaceful coexistence took account of the prevailing technological, political and strategic environment: 'Recognizing the danger of a nuclear war with the United States, Krushchev needed to establish an ideological basis for the existence of a long-term relationship between communism and capitalism that would not lead to war.'[54]

Khrushchev's peaceful coexistence was not to be a tactical and short term expedient, as under Lenin and later Malenkov. He made two important qualifications to Marxist–Leninist doctrine: the thesis of the inevitability of war was rejected and the argument that Communism would be achieved by non-violent, perhaps even parliamentary, means was advanced. War was no longer a fatalistic inevitability, but Marxist–Leninist orthodoxy was modified to accommodate the theory that the mighty social and political forces of Communism would stop the imperialists from launching a war. There was an increasing possibility of the non-violent transformation to socialism, and socialism without revolution might be an important way to Communism. In effect, in the thermonuclear age, the Soviet leaders recognized that a new doctrine was necessary. Military force was to be used only *in extremis* – to prevent a corrosion of Soviet security – as it was in Hungary in 1956 and later in Czechoslovakia in 1968. The Soviet estimate of the West's defensive attitude appeared to be confirmed by the low-key response to the Soviet repression of the revolt in Hungary. At the 20th Congress of the CPSU Khrushchev argued:

There is, of course, a Marxist–Leninist precept, that wars

are inevitable as long as imperialism exists. This precept was evolved at a time when (1) imperialism was an all-embracing world system, and (2) the social and political forces which did not want war were weak, poorly organised, and hence unable to compel the imperialist to renounce war.

People usually take only one aspect of the question and examine only the economic basis of wars under imperialism. This is not enough. War is not only an economic phenomenon. Whether there is to be war or not depends in large measure on the correlation of class, political forces, the degree of organisation and the awareness and determination of the people. Moreover, in certain conditions the struggle waged by progressive social and political forces may play a decisive role. Hitherto the state of affairs was such that the forces that did not want war and opposed it were poorly organised and lacked the means to check the schemes of the war makers. Thus it was before the First World War, when the main force opposed to the threat of war – the world proletariat – was disorganised by the treachery of the leaders of the Second International. Thus it was on the eve of the Second World War, when the Soviet Union was the only country that pursued an active peace policy, when the other great powers to all intents and purposes encouraged the aggressors, and the right-wing social-democratic leaders had split the labour movement in the capitalist countries.

In that period this precept was absolutely correct. In the present time, however, the situation has changed radically. Now there is a world camp of socialism which has become a mighty force. In this camp the peace forces find not only the moral, but also the material means to prevent aggression. Moreover, there is a large group of other countries with a population running into many hundreds of millions which are actively working to avert war. Their labour movement in the capitalist countries has today become a tremendous force. The movement of peace supporters has sprung up and developed into a powerful factor. In the circumstances certainly the Leninist precept that so long as imperialism exists, the economic basis giving rise to wars will also be preserved remains in force. That is why we must display the greatest vigilance. As long as capitalism survives in the world, reactionary forces representing the interests of the capitalist monopolies will continue their drive towards military gambles and aggression and may try to unleash war. But war is not fatalistically inevitable . . .

. . . the present situation offers the working class in a number of capitalist countries a real opportunity to unite the overwhelming majority of the people under its leadership and to secure the transfer of its basic means of production into the hands of the people. The right wing bourgeois parties and their governments are suffering bankruptcy with increasing frequency. In these circumstances the working class, by rallying around itself the working peasantry, intelligentsia, all patriotic forces, and resolutely repulsing the opportunist elements who are incapable of giving up the policy of compromise with the capitalists and landlords, is in a position to defeat the reactionary forces opposed to the interests of the people, to capture a stable majority in parliament, and transform the latter from an organ of bourgeois democracy into a genuine instrument of the people's will.[55]

The fear of nuclear war, and the realization that the opposing camp also feared it, led to the basic strategy of deterrence being somewhat expanded in the years following 1956 to also encompass a strategy of counter-deterrence; both strategies were to lend themselves to the achievement of foreign policy objectives within peaceful coexistence. The theory of counter-deterrence involved the use of Soviet nuclear forces to deter the United States from resorting to its nuclear deterrent as a way of preventing the Soviet use of economic, political, subversive or even proxy limited war instruments to achieve foreign policy objectives: 'Nuclear power was relegated to the desperate, defensive, last resort should there be no alternative (deterrence) but military instruments remained important means of offensive infiltration and pressure. Their chief role has been to counter and neutralise the Western use of nuclear power to prevent Communist gains (counter deterrence).'[56] The use of non-military instruments, or the threatened use of nuclear weapons, are all viewed as quite legitimate in the peaceful coexistence of Khrushchev, depending on the correlation of forces between the Soviets and the opposition. Deterrence was accepted because the current correlation of forces was against the Soviet Union, and the only alternative in orthodox Marxism–Leninism was thermonuclear world war. However, if the world balance of power, or particular circumstances, favoured the Soviet Union, then the new dogma allowed offensive action – one step backwards when the occasion demanded it, and two steps forwards when the circumstances allowed it. Bearing this in mind, one can better comprehend the series of retreats and offensives which constitute Soviet foreign policy since 1956: 'The relation of forces between the USSR and the capitalist world is the basic determinant of Soviet foreign policy.'[57]

In the minds of the Soviet policy makers peaceful coexistence applies to relations between states, not classes, so the ideological struggle continues. In his February 1956 address Khrushchev heralded Soviet support for 'wars of national liberation' in the decolonizing world, and he was to reiterate this support throughout his ten years of office. Such conflicts, in Moscow's eyes, constituted struggles between classes or states, and support for subversive or guerrilla movements did not contradict peaceful coexistence, but were legitimized by the doctrine. In contrast to containment, peaceful coexistence – in spite of some emphasis on cooperation between East and West if the correlation of forces, whether political, economic, social or military, demand it – is fundamentally a non-status quo doctrine. Marxism–Leninism sees the correlation of forces as inherently unstable and there to be manipulated to a state's advantage.[58] Illustrations of an attempt by the Soviet Union to use a favourable correlation of forces, in this instance strategic, to its political advantage, were the Berlin crises of 1958–61. The launching of Sputnik in 1957 demonstrated Soviet ICBM capability, and created considerable anxiety in the United States over homeland vulnerability and a 'missile gap' between the US and the Soviet Union much to Moscow's advantage. Moscow did nothing to allay such fears, even though it was not at that stage pressing ahead with a large ICBM construction programme.

November 1958 saw the initiation of the confrontation over Berlin, which was to be the central issue of the Cold War between 1958 and the Cuban missile crisis of 1962. The Soviet Union claimed that it no longer recognized obligations assumed under the Potsdam agreement, specifically the provisions relating to Berlin. By threatening to hand the control of the Soviet sector to the East Germans, the Soviets were really saying that they wanted the Western powers out of West Berlin. The West was given six months to comply; if it did not, the Soviets would turn the control of military traffic between West Germany and West Berlin, across the territory of the German Democratic Republic or what the Western powers still insisted was a Soviet zone in East Germany, a state which the Western allies did not recognize, over to the East German government.

NATO supported the claims of the Federal Republic as the only legitimate government of Germany. With the ball in the court of the West, who were in a weak conventional position, the onus would be on them to resist change. The objective was not only to remove the Western Allies from West Berlin, but also to demonstrate the unreliability of the United States' commitment, nuclear and otherwise, thereby alienating the Federal Republic from the United States. The overall result would have been to stabilize the status quo in Europe to Soviet advantage, and divide NATO. If achieved, it would have exceeded any foreign policy success since 1945 and made Khrushchev's domestic position unassailable. Part of this manoeuvre was to convince the West that, considering the risks the Soviets were taking, they must have the means and be prepared to use them. The only effective way the United States could counter a Soviet and East German move in Berlin was by nuclear weapons, but would they do so if they believed the US homeland to be at risk? Everything depended on the Soviet bluff:

> The Soviet leaders could at best simulate the determination to do whatever was necessary to achieve their declared objective, for they did not possess the means to sustain a genuine determination. In order to appear willing to take risks that they knew to be imprudent, the Soviet leaders, among other actions, deliberately conveyed an exaggerated impression of the size and scope of their ICBM programme.[59]

Despite various bellicose statements by Khrushchev, and although the Western allies offered slight concessions just in case capabilities equalled objectives, the Western powers were not prepared to give much without some kind of demonstration of Soviet power. Because of the cooling of the Soviet offensive by the summer of 1959 and the results of United States surveillance, doubts began to be raised about the 'missile gap'. By the time of the Kennedy–Khrushchev summit of May 1961, and the renewed Berlin offensive of mid-1961 with its demand for the conversion of West Berlin into a free city, the 'missile gap' bluff was all but blown. The result was the construction of the Berlin wall on 13 August 1961. Discreetly welcomed by many in the West, it was seen as a *de facto* resolution of the issue, a stabilization of the situation, and a revelation of the Soviet bluff. Two months later Khrushchev officially lifted his Berlin deadline, and thereby closed his political offensive. The Cuban missile crisis of October 1962 was an attempt by the Soviet leader to regain a favourable correlation of forces for the Soviet Union, and salvage his own political position. Faced by overwhelming United States conventional military superiority in the Caribbean, and overall nuclear superiority, the Cuban adventure was doomed to failure.

In October 1964 Khrushchev was removed from office, and the Brezhnev/Kosygin coalition took power in Moscow. However, Khrushchev's peaceful coexistence doctrine survived and continues to this day as the ideological backdrop to and basis for Soviet foreign policy.[60] The new leaders resolved to build up Soviet military and economic strength while avoiding crises such as Berlin and Cuba. In the years since 1964 East–West relations have gone through many cool phases, such as at the height of the United States' military action in the Vietnam War, the Middle East War of October 1973, and the invasion of Afghanistan by the Soviet Union in 1979/80, but peaceful coexistence has never been abandoned. On the eve of Brezhnev's visit to the United States in 1973, *Pravda* reprinted an extract from one of his speeches of six months earlier to celebrate the fiftieth anniversary of the Soviet Union:

> The . . . class struggle of the two systems . . . in the sphere of economics, politics, and, it goes without saying, ideology,

will be continued ... the world outlook and the aims of
socialism are opposed and irreconcilable. But we shall
ensure that this inevitable struggle is transferred to a
channel which does not threaten wars, dangerous conflicts,
and an uncontrolled arms race.[61]

Détente

In Soviet eyes *détente* is not distinct from peaceful coexistence, but
rather it is an instrument of Soviet foreign policy directly derived
from and legitimized by peaceful coexistence. There are three
basic principles to peaceful coexistence and *détente*:

1 the repudiation of nuclear war as a means of resolving
   political disputes between capitalist and socialist countries;
2 the expansion of mutually advantageous cooperation
   between capitalism and socialism; and
3 the recognition of national sovereignty and non-interference
   in the internal affairs of other nations. Unlike most Wester-
   ners Soviet officials do not find this third principle incompati-
   ble with Soviet military and economic support for promising
   'national liberation movements' in Third World countries.[62]

Peaceful coexistence is recognized as a 'general rule'[63] of relations between states with different social systems. *Détente* is the
emphasis given to principle 2 above, and is seen to be a permanent
factor in international relations – a condition resulting from peaceful coexistence rather than a policy *per se*:

In communist theory Brezhnev's *détente* adds nothing to the
concept of peaceful coexistence. But in practice it was to
encompass a much closer degree of cooperation with those
countries which had previously been looked upon as adversaries. It envisioned cooperation in areas of arms control,
trade, crisis settlement, science, technology and more. Brezhnev wanted not just the avoidance of conflict, he needed the
active collaboration of the West.[64]

As well as being an element and extension of peaceful coexistence,
détente is also seen by Moscow as an instrument in support of the

doctrine. Whatever *détente* may be perceived to be in the West, in Soviet eyes it is quite loyal to ideology. At the 25th Congress of the CPSU in 1974 Brezhnev stressed that '*détente* does not in the slightest abolish, nor can it alter, the laws of the class struggle . . . we make no secret of the fact that we see *détente* as the way to create more favourable conditions for peaceful socialist and Communist construction.'[65]

The real distinction between peaceful coexistence and *détente* is not ideological, but the circumstances is in which they are applied. The most recent and lengthy phase of *détente* has occurred against a backdrop of new international, military and economic factors which have induced the United States and the Soviet Union to undertake *détente* in pursuit of their own differing sets of objectives, and to conduct relations at a lower level of tension than during the Cold War period: '*détente* supposes a conscious and deliberate *reduction* of tensions in the central balance . . . whereas cold war assumes a conscious *maintenance* of tensions at a relatively high level.[66] *Détente* assumes a considerable degree of adversarial co-operation, in pursuit of a state's own objectives. As objectives are usually different, then a clash of interests is unlikely. Ideally, the zero-sum mentality of the Cold War is no longer appropriate; a gain for one side is no longer assumed to be a loss for the other. Hence, some limited cooperation is beneficial, particularly given the actual or potential costs of the alternative, which could be all-out competition and perhaps even military conflict.

The most recent phase of *détente*, lasting from 1969 until, some would argue, 1980 or thereabouts has not been the only period of relaxed East–West tensions and adversarial cooperation since 1945, though it has been the longest and most productive. [67] There was an early *détente* in the years 1954–55, following on Stalin's death in March 1953 and during a period of leadership manoeuvring in Moscow. In 1955 there was agreement on the sovereignty and neutrality of Austria; Bonn and Moscow exchanged ambassadors, and a notable summit meeting was held in Geneva in the July when President Eisenhower and the British and French prime ministers met Khrushchev and Bulganin. Nothing of substance was produced by the summit, but the general view was that the resultant atmosphere was conducive to relaxed tensions. The following year the twin crises of Suez and Hungary revived East–

West tensions, which were heightened by the Sputnik achievement of 1957 and the Berlin crisis of 1958–59. Khrushchev's visit to the United States in 1959, in between the Berlin crises of 1958 and 1961, led to expectations of better relations, but the U-2 incident when the United States spy plane was shot down over the Soviet Union in 1960, the breakdown of the Paris summit of that year, and another Berlin crisis, undermined the fragile basis of an East–West accord derived from Khrushchev's visit.

Of the earlier *détentes*, the most productive was that after the Cuban crisis during Khrushchev's period of ascendancy, This was marked by the establishment of the hot line between the Kremlin and the White House, and the signing of the Partial Test Ban Treaty of 1963, banning nuclear tests except those conducted underground. The Soviet Union's deteriorating relations with the People's Republic of China, Khrushchev's desire to control the arms race until the Soviet Union was better placed to compete with the United States, and mounting economic problems, were all compelling factors driving Khrushchev towards *détente* following the *débâcle* of his Cuban adventure in 1962.[68] The removal from the international scene of the two major personalities of *détente* Kennedy and Khrushchev, and the escalation of United States military action in Vietnam by the mid 1960s, brought the final phase of Khrushchevian *détente* to an end. But the factors compelling Khrushchev in such a direction remained extant, and were even more compelling for the Soviet leadership by the end of the 1960s.

The most recent phase of *détente* has its roots in events of 1969. By the end of the decade Brezhnev was established as the predominant political figure in Moscow, a new president was in office in Washington, and developments on the international scene were propitious for a new, more complex and hence perhaps more securely-based phase of East–West *détente* – not merely between the superpowers, but with active West European involvement:

> The crucial year was 1969. Several factors came together to prompt a change of strategy. A new administration in the United States appeared ready to accept the implications of Soviet nuclear might for Washington's previous military superiority. In Moscow, Brezhnev was receptive to the idea that the superpowers should engage in serious arms limita-

tion. In Europe the tentative negotiations for a treaty between West Germany and the Soviet Union renouncing the use of force speeded up in September with the election of Willy Brandt, a man the Russians felt they could trust. Armed clashes between Soviet and Chinese troops in March prompted the Kremlin to think that an improvement of relations with the West could help it to deal more easily with Peking. Finally there was the economic factor. Soviet leaders were becoming increasingly aware that growth rates would soon decline, as the country's labour surplus dried up and it ran out of easily exploitable reserves of raw materials. Continuing difficulties in agriculture were sharpened by a particularly severe winter in 1969 which caused serious shortages of meat. One solution was to abandon the Soviet Union's previous attempts at self-sufficiency and to look to the West for imports, not only of technology and capital, but also food.[69]

Similarly, in Washington, the new administration of Richard Nixon recognized the international environment as conducive to a new approach to East–West relations. The costs of the war in south–east Asia created a reluctance to sustain containment, wherever it might be required. The large defence budgets were seen by many as unbalancing the domestic economy, while among the population at large there was considerable unease over the manpower required to implement the containment strategy. The accretion of Soviet military power throughout the 1960s had produced a situation of crude nuclear parity. Hence, 'Soviet military power could now neutralise the ability of United States military power to deter objectionable Soviet behaviour short of direct threats to the United States itself. New means for affecting Soviet behaviour were required to supplement military deterrence.'[70] Furthermore, the United States' West European allies were aware of the changing international environment, and were enthusiastic to establish a *modus vivendi* in Europe with the Soviet Union. Their reasons were not merely military, but primarily political, economic and social. De Gaulle was inclined to minimize the military threat from the Soviet Union, and believed that a political opening-up to the East would ease tensions throughout Europe. By 1969, after a number of false starts, the Federal Republic of Germany, under an SPD/FDP coalition led by Willy Brandt, wished to regularize the *de facto* postwar political situation in central Europe. Brandt saw it as essential for the self-esteem of the Federal Republic and its international rehabilitation that is should deal on an equal basis with the states of East Europe. The Cold War policies of previous Bonn governments had not recovered lost lands to the east, and it was even less likely that European boundaries would be changed in 1970 than in the 1950s, when a United States superiority in nuclear weapons was backing Adenauer's claims. An easing of political tensions was seen to be of benefit to the millions of Germans living in East Europe and, very importantly, could lead to a major expansion of West German trade in that direction.

The East–West *détente* that was gathering pace in 1969 and 1970 was very different from previous *détentes*. Thoses of 1954–55, 1959 and 1963–64 were essentially bilateral, with the United States and Soviet Union as the predominant actors. This was not so in 1970: not only did major West European participation contribute to a multilateral *détente*, but the People's Republic of China played a vital role in its creation and dynamics. Indeed, without the participation of Peking, the *détente* of the 1970s would have been a very different animal, and might never have taken off in the first instance.

The three major actors in the post-1969 *détente* were the United States, the Soviet Union and the PRC – a trilateral *détente* in contrast to the occasional bilateral *détentes* of the previous twenty years. The attraction of this relationship for the United States was the pivotal position that it enjoyed. Washington pursued *détente* with both Moscow and Peking, but there was no third side to the triangle – there was no Moscow–Peking *détente*. As a result the United States' 'options, leverage and diplomatic mobility' were maximized.[71] Throughout the 1970s there was no prospect, even after the death of Mao Tse Tung in 1976, of a Sino–Soviet *rapprochement*. In addition to long Chinese memories of Soviet abuse of Chinese Communist Party interests, the disputes over territory and ideology were intractable, and both sides had a deep-seated psychological fear, bordering on paranoia, of the other. There is no doubt that the Sino-US *rapprochement* of the early 1970s, and

Richard Nixon's visit to Peking in February 1972, greatly alarmed the Soviet Union, and encouraged Brezhnev to support *détente* with the United States. In the Pacific area both the Soviet Union and the PRC hoped to use United States military power as a counterweight to the other. The resulting leverage allowed the United States to put considerable pressure on Moscow to influence North Vietnamese behaviour in the peace negotiations leading to the 1973 settlement of the Vietnam War and to the US military withdrawal.[72] The gain for Moscow was Washington's agreement to a package of arms control treaties, economic and credit agreements between the superpowers and, perhaps most important of all to the Soviet psyche, Washington's acknowledgement of the Soviet Union as a military equal and a state with which it could conduct negotiations and reach agreements. To many of the ruling elite in the Soviet Union, with memories stretching back to the Revolution, the importance of being treated as an equal to the United States in the eyes of the world should not be underestimated. This may explain why the Soviet Union has so valued *détente*, and sustained the concept throughout the 1970s, even though enthusiasm for it in the United States was in evident decline from 1976. Indeed, during the 1976 presidential election campaign President Ford instructed his staff not to use the word, so discredited was the concept in that country.

A major weakness in the superpower *détente* relationship was the distinct views that both sides had on the scope and nature of *détente*. As mentioned above, the superpowers had different short term objectives, but fundamentally both saw *détente* as protecting and advancing their ideological perspectives. For the Soviet Union it emphasized the cooperative aspects of peaceful coexistence; for the United States it replaced containment and compensated for the loss of military superiority:

> Nixon and Kissinger were clear about the meaning they attached to '*détente*' . . . they viewed it as yet another in a long series of attempts to contain the power and influence of the Soviet Union, but one based on a new combination of pressures and inducements that would, if successful, convince the Russians that it was in their own best interests to be contained.[73]

The United States was inclined to see *détente* as a policy rather than a condition. Both sides were in agreement on lowering tensions and avoiding open conflict which could escalate to nuclear war, though the United States saw relaxation and cooperation in one area as a reward to be withdrawn if the Soviets misbehaved elsewhere – a policy of linkage. Washington's geostrategic perspective was global and universal, whereas the Soviet perspective of *détente* is much more regional and functional, and Moscow most certainly does not accept that regional *détente* in Europe or functional *détente* in arms control should inhibit Soviet support for the class struggle in the Third World. This divergence of views between the superpowers raised particular difficulties for the West Europeans.

As we have seen, *détente* is a product of the Cold War and, as with the Cold War, the United States and the West European allies have pursued the *détente* process in different though often complementary ways, and supported asymmetrical perspectives of its primary qualities and purposes. Since the early 1960s the United States has conceptualized *détente* as a military and a global process, with the focus of policy makers in all the administrations since John Kennedy on the Soviet Union's military capabilities and on its military threat, and on how *détente* could best serve United States military–security objectives. Obviously military *détente* has not been pursued to the exclusion of political and economic *détente* – for example, in the early years of the Carter administration human rights assumed a high foreign policy profile – but invariably the other *détentes* have taken second place to military *détente* when military security objectives were at risk or when the other *détentes* could be used as instruments to further military *détente*: for example, the Nixon administration's political *détente* with the PRC. On the other hand, the West European *détente* has been conceptualized primarily as a political process, with attention focused on assessments of the political intentions of the Soviet Union in Europe and the political threat posed. The West Europeans have not viewed *détente* exclusively in political terms, with military and economic *détente* receiving consistent support; but economic *détente*, for example, has clearly been used as an instrument for political *détente*, while disappointing results in the field of military *détente* have been utilized, not as a means to discredit *détente*, but as all the more reason to pursue a relaxation of political tensions.

In the aftermath of the Korean War the United States conceptualized containment as a military strategy and the Cold War as a global conflict. *Détente* has likewise been conceptualized in global and military terms. Undoubtedly, the superpower bilateral codification of *détente* has primarily been of a military nature, and where it has not been purely military the salient military elements have received the most public attention and political acclaim. In the *détente* of 1963–64, the hot line between Washington and Moscow and the Partial Test Ban Treaty between the United States (with Great Britain) and the Soviet Union received most attention. Since 1969, at the heart of *détente* for all the administrations in Washington have been SALT 1 and the ABM Treaty of 1972, the military elements of the Treaty on Basic Principles of Relations between the United States and the USSR of 1972, the Vladivostok accords of 1974, and SALT II.[74] In the early 1970s a vain attempt at political, military and economic linkage took place, supported in its early manifestations by Henry Kissinger and later by conservative elements in Congress; but, faced with a divisible interpretation of *détente* by the Soviet Union and domestic obstacles to a foreign policy consensus at home in the wake of the Vietnam War, linkage was soon abandoned as a major policy instrument.[75] *Détente* in the United States soon came to be judged by the success or otherwise of superpower arms control, rather than arms control being accepted as a component, albeit a very important one, of the overall *détente* process.[76] In the United States the military perspective was reinforced as, throughout the 1970s, *détente* was increasingly measured in military terms. Dismay grew at the modernization and build-up of Soviet strategic nuclear, naval, and conventional military capabilities. The Soviet-sponsored Cuban military activities in Africa and the Soviet invasion of Afghanistan were seen to be contrary to the spirit, if not the codified letter, of superpower *détente*. Ironically, the growing dissatisfaction with the process, as measured in military terms, contributed to the strength of conservative feeling in the United States against the Carter administration's SALT II agreement which, when judged by many to be unsatisfactory, contrary to official advice, was held up as further evidence of the unequal nature of superpower *détente*.

As with the Cold War, the West European response to *détente* was and is essentially political. In the early years of the Cold War, particularly following the Communist *coup d'état* in Czechoslovakia in 1948, the West European states encouraged not only United States economic and political support but also a military commitment to West European security. Convinced by the West Europeans of the military threat, the United States took up the military burden, but in the early post-Korean years the Europeans then returned to a primarily political appreciation of the threat. De Gaulle's opening-up to the East in the early 1960s was based upon an appreciation of the relative military security of Europe and hence the opportunity for France to take the political initiative. The Ostpolitik of the Federal Republic which gathered pace in the 1960s and, despite (or because of) the invasion of Czechoslovakia in 1968, blossomed in the 1970s, was rooted in an awareness of West German military security through membership of NATO, but was in itself a political process. The hallmarks of Ostpolitik, the Moscow, Warsaw and inter-German treaties were primarily political settlements, aimed at removing political tensions. Similarly, the concomitant Quadri-partite Agreement on Berlin, negotiated between the four occupying powers, was a political settlement, considerably reducing tensions in Europe's most dangerous potential crisis spot. It could be argued that the Mutual Force Reduction talks in Vienna focus on the East–West military balance in Europe and so fall into the category of military *détente*. Concern over manpower and tanks do form the basis of discussion, but the MFR talks began in the first place as a quid pro quo from Moscow in order to achieve NATO agreement to the Soviet suggestion for a European security conference. The West Europeans welcomed force reduction talks because it would ease political pressure from the Senate in Washington on the Nixon administration to withdraw troops from Europe. The MFR talks have continued for well over a decade – they were not postponed or cancelled when the Soviet Union invaded Afghanistan – because they serve a political purpose: they provide a mechanism for multilateral East–West rather than superpower bilateral dialogue. Furthermore, it has been suggested that the Soviet Union has little desire to reach agreement because the withdrawal of some United States forces could have the political effect of encouraging a new bout of either West European integration or West European nationalism.[77] The Final Act of the Conference on Security and Cooperation in Europe of 1975 contained military clauses relating to the use of force and to confidence-building measures, but the emphasis was on political and economic *détente*. In return for the legitimization of the post 1945 frontiers in East Europe, the West received assurances on sovereign rights, human rights, and economic and scientific cooperation. The human rights expectations have not been fulfilled, but the West European continental states, especially the Federal Republic of Germany, have maximized the other aspects of political and economic *détente* facilitated by the Helsinki Final Act.

The West Europeans have certainly welcomed the bilateral SALT process and attributed to it great significance in terms of superpower *détente*, but while condemning Soviet-supported adventures in the Third World, the Soviet arms build-up and the invasion of Afghanistan, the political objectives of *détente* (including the economic aspect) have been accorded priority. Indeed, for the West Europeans *détente* has served a distinctly European and political function, affordable in part because of the military and global perspective of the United States. Hence there is an awareness in West Europe, which acts as an in-built break on United States–West European discord, that the twin perspectives of *détente* should not be permitted to diverge too much. But, notwithstanding the preferences of some West European leaders, the former colonial powers of a presently welfare-orientated, introspective West Europe cannot afford a global vision for a mix of economic, sociopolitical and, most acutely, geopolitical reasons. In Washington the global–military perspective was and is seen to be essential to national interest, just as the more limited geopolitical perspective of the West European states is perceived as essential to West European national interests.

Since the heady days of the Helsinki Final Act, *détente* has suffered a steep decline, primarily through dissatisfaction in the West, especially in the United States. Washington has not found it easy to give up nuclear superiority and accept parity. Nor has the United States been able to come to terms with radical changes in the Third World or the continued resistance of the Soviet Union to meaningful internal change. Trade between the two superpowers, after impressive surges in the early 1970s, has been severely stifled since the mid 1970s, very much as a result of the Congressional insistence on linking trade *détente* with progress on human rights in the Soviet Union.[78]

The election of Ronald Reagan to the White House in 1979 and his commitment to a United States military build-up, the continuing Soviet military build-up, the failure of attempts at arms control agreements at global strategic and European theatre level, and the deepest decline in East–West relations since the Cuban missile crisis – all of these factors raise the question – does *détente* still exist? The ideological confrontation continues. That is plain for all to see in the mid-1980s, and is more evident than at any time since the death of Stalin. But such ideological differences do not invalidate *détente*. Indeed, the opposite is the case. Ideological confrontation is inherent in the Soviet view of *détente*, based as it is on peaceful coexistence. For the United States, ideological containment, if not accommodation and even subversion, was always a *détente* objective. *Détente* is still with us because, overriding the ideological conflict, there is an awareness that the superpowers remain adversary partners committed to avoiding open conflict. This reality has not changed since 1973, when Henry Kissinger argued: 'The Soviet Union and we are in a unique partnership. We are at one and the same time adversaries and partners in the preservation of peace.'[79]

Regardless of political differences, there remains less likelihood of superpower nuclear war now than before 1969. There is an overwhelming international expectation of and enthusiasm for the success of the major manifestation of *détente* – arms control talks and agreements. This is especially so amongst the West European allies, and there is evidence that such feelings are prevalent also in East Europe. Presently East and West are talking at the Conference on Disarmament in Europe in Stockholm, at the Mutual Force Reduction talks in Vienna and at nuclear arms control talks in Geneva, and in Europe trade between East and West continues at historically high levels for the postwar era. East–West relations may be at a low ebb, but international security, especially in Europe, is much more stable and less brittle than in 1949, or 1959 or 1969, and there persists the fundamental appreciation of mutual interests between the two superpowers whose military might meets in the heart of Europe. Between 1972 and 1980 there were five United States–Soviet summits, more than in the previous fifty years of US–Soviet relations. In the 1970s more than two dozen agreements between the superpowers were signed, and the ground rules for superpower conduct *vis-à-vis* each other were established. These ground rules remain extant. In Europe the Ostpolitik treaties of the early 1970s have produced an unprecedented era of international security and harmony in what was previously one of the most sensitive areas of East–West competition.

Pervading most of the doctrinal pronunciations in both East and West over the past thirty years, and at the heart of the military element of *détente* in the 1970s, has been an acute awareness that both superpowers and blocs are living ,in a nuclear environment. Superseding all other considerations, the reason for such cautious and strategic behaviour in the face of opposing ideologies has been the desire to sustain foreign policy objectives while avoiding nuclear war. Containment, peaceful coexistence and *détente* have had, at their very core, a profound sense of the ultimate hopelessness of nuclear conflict.

3

The Nuclear Environment

As never before in the history of mankind, all the societies which constitute the international system today are vulnerable to terrible devastation. This does not mean that cataclysmic nuclear war is imminent or inevitable. It is clearly neither imminent nor inevitable. Given the prevailing arms balance between the nuclear powers, the level of political tension and the stability of the political leaderships, nuclear war seems highly improbable – but it is not impossible.

If nuclear war were to occur, no state, no matter how powerful and influential, could remain immune by its own volition or create an invulnerable defence. Since the advent of the atomic bomb, offensive weapons – for instance atomic bombers and later ballistic missiles equipped with multiple warheads – have been in the ascendancy. The United States is currently engaged in a major programme of research, the Strategic Defence Initiative (SDI), in pursuit of effective ballistic missile defence (BMD). Such are the immense technological problems to be overcome that there is little reason to expect the eventual deployment of a leak-proof BMD system around NATO, or even the United States alone. A major strategic problem for BMD is that it appears, at present, much cheaper for an adversary to multiply warheads to 'swamp' BMD than for the defender to take compensatory defensive measures. Even if SDI does bear fruit and provide a cost-effective, leak-proof BMD for NATO or just the United States, BMD is not effective against cruise missiles and manned bombers. The state of the technological art suggests that it may be possible to provide effective point BMD in the protection of, for instance, command centres and ICBM silos, but societies will remain vulnerable to nuclear devastation for the foreseeable future.

In sharp contrast to the other major revolutions in military organization and technology in the modern era – the mass warfare of the Napoleonic age and the industrialized warfare of the First and Second World Wars – the advent of nuclear weapons has raised the prospect of no escape from societal devastation in the event of major hostilities between the great powers in the contemporary world. The First and Second World Wars brought the battlefield to the homeland, and defeat in war could threaten drastic changes in the form of one's society. War between nuclear powers threatens the very existence of society itself:

> Nuclear war does not fit into the moral categories that are ordinarily applied to war. It undercuts familiar political ways of thinking by escaping the bounds of the very definition of war. Similarly, it threatens to shatter cultural mechanisms for coping with death by destroying everything that makes symbolic immortality possible. The difference between the wars in which the two previous modern military revolutions appeared and a full-scale nuclear war is the difference between destruction and annihilation. It is the difference between the end of an era and the end of a culture. Nuclear weapons, unlike all other weapons known to man, 'have the power to make everything into nothing'.[1]

Such vulnerability has been a major feature of East–West relations since 1949, when the Soviet Union demonstrated its atomic status as a military power. The qualified exception to this general rule was the geostrategic situation of the United States in the period before 1957. Betweeen 1945 and 1949 the United States had an atomic monopoly; between the years 1949 and 1957 the American homeland was deemed to be relatively invulnerable to attack from external powers. Such were the distances between the American heartland and the Soviet Union, and such were the limited ranges of the Soviet delivery vehicles, that there was considerable confidence that American society was invulnerable to a devastating Soviet atomic attack. The Soviet Union was not in a similar fortunate position. The United States' atomic and nuclear forces have been based forward, in West Europe, since 1948, within striking range of the western districts of the Soviet Union and its social, economic and industrial heart. In the years 1948 to 1957 Soviet security was rooted in the notion of the preponderant conventional power of the Red Army holding 'Europe hostage for United States good behaviour'.[2] While such a strategy was not clearly articulated by the Soviet Union, it was implicit in the deployment and build-up of Soviet military power in Europe. Indeed, it could be argued that it was under this conventional military umbrella that the Soviet Union strove to develop its nuclear military power.

However, in 1957 the United States discovered itself to be, or soon to be, as vulnerable as the Soviet Union to nuclear devastation. The successful launching of the Sputnik satellite demonstrated that the Soviet Union had acquired an intercontinental ballistic missile capability. The direct military consequence was that the United States homeland was open to attack:

> No event focussed popular attention on America's vulnerabilities to attack more than the launching of the world's first artificial earth satellite, *Sputnik I*, by the Soviet Union on 4 October 1957. It brought home the fact that the United States no longer enjoyed invulnerability to the ravages of war. The peoples of Western Europe were familiar with the effects of aerial bombardment and were already growing accustomed to being well within the range of Soviet bombers and missiles. Before the capability to destroy the United States provided the Russians with a retaliatory option, the Western Europeans had served as a hostage. Now Americans also began to suffer the uncomfortable sensation of being candidates for annihilation in the event of total war.[3]

A further shock to the American psyche, which enhanced the feelings of vulnerability, was that the Soviet Union had leapt ahead of the United States in missile technology. Whereas the US had devoted most of its resources to the development of a long-range bomber force, the Soviet Union had concentrated on developing a missile capability and had started research and development in this field before the United States.

There was considerable anxiety in the US that a 'missile gap' between it and the Soviet Union had developed, clearly favouring the Soviets. In fact, the Soviet Union chose not to mass produce ICBMs until the mid-1960s, by which time the United States was far ahead in missile numbers. But in the closing years of the second Eisenhower administration it was clear that the United States could no longer assume itself to be somehow detached from the military–strategic environment of the Old World. The North American continent had become as vulnerable to nuclear holocaust as its allies and adversaries in Europe and throughout the international system. This novel international environment has added new dimensions to the prospect of war and the reality of peace between the nuclear alliance blocs of the developed world. Outside the developed world a tragic number of traditional wars have been waged. These wars have been pursued in an environment where the probability of the introduction of nuclear weapons by patron states from the developed world was not high. In the single recent instance of a war in the developing world where it suddenly looked as though a nuclear element could be introduced into the conflict – the October 1973 war in the Middle East, which will be examined later in this chapter – the character of the war changed and the longer-term political consequences were dramatic.

War in the nuclear environment

> For a generation, the relevant elites of both the USA and USSR have agreed that an unlimited strategic nuclear war would be a disaster of immense proportions.[4]

In the United States there is general agreement in high government and academic circles that in an all-out nuclear war there would be no winners, only losers. In the 1950s Khrushchev and Malenkov were inclined, on occasions, to express similar views.[5] But in the contemporary Soviet Union the policy elite are loath to admit to such realities and to deny any prospect of eventual victory over the adversary. 'Not to believe this would mean that the most basic processes of history, on which Soviet ideology and political legitimacy are founded, could be derailed by the technological works of man and the caprice of a historically doomed opponent.'[6] It is for reasons of ideology, and social and political control, that the Soviet Union has devoted massive resources to ineffective and futile civil defence in some of their major cities. Officially the leadership clings to the notion that there would be some sort of victory resulting from a major strategic nuclear exchange with the West, but they are very vague as to what constitutes 'victory'. It is on record that many of the Soviet policy-making elite have recognized the catastrophe that nuclear war would bring, and they 'do not seem to have any illusions about their nation being able to survive or win a nuclear war in any meaningful sense of the terms'.[7] In Soviet strategic doctrine there is a distinction between declaratory doctrine and practical doctrine. Though the official ideology demands the ultimate triumph, numerous statements from the highest policy-makers provide evidence that there are grave doubts as to the utility of nuclear weapons as a practical instrument of war and acute anxieties as to the horrendous costs of such an exercise. Indeed, the accumulating scientific evidence, from both sides of the Iron Curtain, that a major nuclear exchange would in all probability produce such ecological damage – the so-called 'nuclear winter' – that all of mankind and its natural environment would be liable to extinction, demonstrates the absurdity of the Soviet Union's reluctance to deny any prospect of meaningful victory in an all-out nuclear war.[8]

In a conflict between nuclear states, in the nuclear era, one side could conceivably 'win' battles in the sense that the military forces of the adversary would suffer greater losses on the battlefield and would either be destroyed or have to abandon their positions. It is also conceivable that one side could 'win' a major nuclear war, in so far that on the military balance sheet more of the 'victor's' forces might survive, the adversary might be denied its objectives, and a potential political, geostrategic or economic advantage might have been attained. But the very existence of the 'victor' would remain threatened and at severe risk if the 'loser', on the battlefield or in the war, possessed an invulnerable, retaliatory second-strike nuclear force. If the costs of the war were found to be unbearable or if the defeated state were in ruins after the defeat, then the defeated could exact awful punishment on the 'victor'. Such retribution from the grave makes a victory meaningless.

The United States, the Soviet Union, Britain and France have taken advantage of the advent and development of the most invulnerable and powerful second-strike system – the ballistic-missile nuclear submarine (SSBN) – to procure secure second-strike deterrents. A state may be said to possess an invulnerable second-strike system when its military forces can ride out a massive counter-force first strike from an adversary and still be able to present a credible, devastating, proportionate response against the adversary. In this regard vulnerable land-based missiles – even though hardened silos do add a considerable degree of survivability – and land- or sea-based bomber fleets which are very exposed to pre-emptive attacks and about which there are grave doubts as to penetrability, given modern air defence systems, are not the ideal systems for second-strike purposes. It is the deep-diving, relatively undetectable, long-range ballistic missile-firing submarine which posits an assured second-strike capability. Given the relative inaccuracy of SLBMs in the 1960s and 1970s, SSBNs were usually identified as counter-city systems with the potential, come what may, of holding an adversary's society hostage to good behaviour. Indeed, many liberals in the community of scholars and analysts in the West who look at international security, in particular the nuclear aspects, argue that the goal of peace-loving governments should be to put as much of the deterrent into submarines as prudently possible, thereby ensuring and enhancing assured retaliation, and to remove as many destabilizing land-based systems as possible.[9] Land-based nuclear systems are destabilizing because first, they are more accurate and hence could tempt use as first-strike weapons or, second, they could tempt a first-strike from the other side because of their vulnerability. However, a major problem with this proposal is that some United States systems, apart from SSBNs, might be required in a first-use mode in support of extended deterrence, particularly in Europe. In this mode accurate land-based missiles or bomber fleets could be required not as a high risk-taking, bolt-out-of-the-blue disarming first strike, but in support of conventional forces in a conflict already under way and initiated by the adversary.

Allies of the United States presently offered nuclear guarantees would not be reassured by a US policy only to deploy, or to severely limit nuclear forces to, an assured-destruction second-strike deterrent. And it is only fair to say that the allies would be equally alarmed by a major move in the opposite direction! A further problem for such seemingly sensible proposals is that the new generation of SLBMs on delivery systems such as Trident II are accurate enough to fulfil a first-strike counter-force role, as well as subsequent other strikes against a whole range of targets below the threshold of a counter-city strike. Nevertheless, SSBNs remain the repositories of assured proportionate second-strike capability. The SSBN forces of the United States and the Soviet Union could each destroy the other state as a functioning society, while the SSBN forces of France and Britain, although delivering but a fraction of the warheads of the superpowers, could exact a cost from the Soviet Union, the most likely adversary, far in excess of the value to that state of the destruction of Britain or France. For instance, at a conservative estimate, it is reckoned that one British Polaris SSBN strike could kill 20 million Russians and destroy four or five major Soviet cities.

In the search for an escape from the universal horror of nuclear war, efforts have been made by civilian defence thinkers and military planners, especially in the West, to concoct limited nuclear war strategies. The notion is that if the conflict is over limited objectives, then it is inappropriate to use disproportionate nuclear means. Nuclear war need not escalate – that is the hope. Devastation can be contained, given the appropriate political context. The threat of greater nuclear devastation, it is hoped, may act as a deterrent to escalation by either combatant.

The theories of limited nuclear war came to the fore in the late 1950s in response to a particular European problem. The Warsaw Pact was perceived to be superior in conventional arms. The West European states in NATO, for a mix of political and economic reasons, were unwilling or unable to raise enough conventional forces to provide a credible prospect of holding off a Warsaw Pact attack against West Europe without a relatively early resort to nuclear weapons. Yet there was considerable reluctance in the West to accept that there should be such a rapid escalation to all-out nuclear war so early in the conflict. United States administrations in the 1960s were particularly reluctant to accept such a strategy, as the American homeland became increasingly vulnerable to Soviet retaliation. Europeans as well were inclined to raise doubts as to the efficacy of massive retaliation. Apart from many other considerations, there was the question of US commitment to such a course of action. A classic question often postulated was: 'Would any American president seriously risk sacrificing New York and Los Angeles by launching a major nuclear attack on the Soviet bloc because of a Warsaw Pact thrust into West Germany – especially if it was in the early days or hours of the conflict? The miniaturization of atomic and nuclear weapons seemed to provide a kind of answer to this strategic conundrum. Small, low-yield nuclear weapons, with relatively limited collateral damage, would be deployed in West Europe: these would be a proportionate nuclear response to a major Warsaw Pact conventional attack. Some extra rungs would be added to the ladder of escalation, and the United States president would be given some limited options. Deterrence against war in central Europe would retain a distinct nuclear element, seen by the Europeans to make war less likely in the first instance and to entangle the United States in European defence should war break out, without running the immediate risk of escalation to total war – a threat of diminishing credibility from any United States president, whose homeland was increasingly vulnerable to the most awful destruction.

So from the late 1950s, tactical or battlefield nuclear weapons were deployed in West Europe, and a number of eminent US strategic analysts popularized and supported the strategy.[10] United States administrations of the past twenty-five years have been committed to a general military strategy of flexible response at conventional and nuclear level, giving decision-makers as many options as possible in the event of a crisis. Since 1967 flexible response has been the official strategy of NATO, an important element being limited nuclear war if NATO is attacked and conventional forces face the prospect of defeat. Over the past twenty years advances in Western military technology appear to have made such a strategy all the more feasible. Decreasing warhead yields, improving accuracy, improving command, control and communication facilities, a vast decrease in the time taken to retarget warheads, and the advent of multiple-warhead missiles – all these have, in theory, greatly increased the range of targets and their vulnerability to limited nuclear attack in war. Limited nuclear war strategy has been accorded a major role in Western deterrence and defence strategy. In the 1980s land-based ICBMs in the United States can be retargeted so quickly and with such accuracy that some are assigned a role in a putative war in central Europe.

Does limited nuclear war provide an escape from the universal holocaust? If one lived in the warzone, be it in central Europe or elsewhere, the difference between limited and all-out nuclear exchange could be marginal and of little significance. For the wider world, there are two crucial questions: (1) in an East–West nuclear conflict, will the Soviets agree to play the limited war game and, (2) even if they do, can nuclear war be controlled anyway?

For Western strategists the Soviet attitude to limited war in Europe is extremely perplexing. Officially, in the early 1960s, Soviet military doctrine did not recognize the possibility of restraint in warfare in Europe. Indeed, it did not recognize the conventional/nuclear firebreak, and the argument was that large conventional forces were required to replace the heavy losses caused by nuclear war. At this time conventional forces were but part of general Soviet war-fighting capabilities and, given the value of the objectives in a European war, deliberate restraint was seen to be impossible and impracticable. Just before the fall of Khrushchev some Soviet military writings began to discuss the prospects of a conventional-arms-only war in Europe, retaining nuclear weapons perhaps only for later use. By the mid-1960s there were two divergent views in Soviet military doctrine on the conventional/nuclear distinction, but the dominant trend was that conventional war would be but an element of general war where the complete range of weapons in the Soviet arsenal would be used. Similarly, in discussion of any tactical/strategic nuclear firebreak in a European war, Soviet writers, with very few exceptions, have insisted that such a distinction is meaningless and impossible. In the 1960s the Soviet assertion was that the introduction of tactical nuclear weapons would inevitably lead to rapid escalation and general nuclear war. At these lower levels of warfare one can guess at the reasons for the reluctance of the Soviets to contemplate limited warfare in Europe. Perhaps such a total view of war helped to deter further Western pressures on the East; perhaps it was seen to add psychologically to the influence derived from the preponderant military force deployed throughout East Europe; or perhaps it reflected the Soviet Union's genuine lack of confidence in their command, control and communication capabilities in pursuing a war in what would be an intensely hostile environment.[11]

Not only has the Soviet Union displayed an official reluctance to play the limited war game at tactical/theatre level, but they reject any notion of limited strategic nuclear war. So while in the 1980s the United States' strategic nuclear war planners may think in terms of first, second, third, fourth and fifth strikes against a whole range of Soviet targets in a strategic nuclear war, moving slowly in a carefully controlled manner up the escalatory ladder, the Soviets insist that they would not be playing the same game. Yet the Soviet Union now deploys a range of strategic nuclear weaponry, and has organized its command, control and communication capabilities in such a manner that it would allow some degree of limited strategic nuclear war, given favourable circumstances. Again the dominant view is that any nuclear war would quickly become all-out nuclear war, but some ambiguity as to actual as distinct from declaratory Soviet intentions remains:

> In fact, the Soviet military seem to be trying to have it both ways, for it is commonly asserted that even very limited nuclear exchanges will inevitably escalate to all-out levels of destruction. Yet, Soviet doctrine continues to assert that massive strategic nuclear exchanges may be followed by a long and ultimately decisive 'conventional' war. This leads directly to requirements not only for substantial nuclear forces but for large and diverse conventional capabilities to fight a war – a war seemingly not much affected by the potential exchange of thousands of nuclear weapons. The solution to this paradox may be found in considering the

different audiences to which such arguments may be addressed, as well as the different purposes which they may be intended to serve. The views set forth above can be read as intended for internal consumption (perhaps even for remaining strands of 'radical or modern' thought within the armed forces themselves). It may be seen as shoring up the barriers against a kind of Malenkovian–Khrushchevian revisionism that has been associated with attempts to cut Soviet defence budgets. The argument on the inevitability of escalation, on the other hand, is more plausibly interpreted as intending to strengthen deterrence by persuading Americans that there is nothing to be gained from limited nuclear war strategies. We should also, of course, keep in mind the additional requirements of the Soviet defence posture, aimed at securing the fruits of World War II in Eastern Europe and maintaining adequate capabilities on other land borders of the Soviet State, most notably the long border with China.[12]

Even assuming, in a European conflict, that the two superpowers arrived at a tacit agreement to recognize some constraint on the use of nuclear weapons, could such an arrangement be put into practice? The outstanding problems in this regard are that of political and technical command, control and communication. First there is the problem of political command and control. Would the other European nuclear powers play the game? In geostrategic and demographic terms Britain and France are highly unsuited to limited nuclear war. In contrast to the nuclear superpowers, Britain and France do not occupy large land masses, population density is much higher, and most military and other possible targets are very close to major cities. For instance, two or three major counter-force strikes against targets such as Faslane, Rosyth and Greenham Common would produce immense collateral damage. The official role of the British independent nuclear deterrent is to retaliate against Soviet cities, including Moscow, in such circumstances; officially French nuclear forces are committed to massive retaliation against Soviet cities in the event of Soviet nuclear strikes on France, no matter if in superpower perspectives such strikes are 'limited'.

Another aspect of the political problem of controlled nuclear war in Europe is that the United States has not forsworn a nuclear attack on the Soviet homeland in the event of a Soviet offensive against West Europe, even if US territory and servicemen are not initially involved. Indeed, the United States consistently reaffirms its nuclear commitment to West European defence and its resolve to use nuclear weapons based in Europe against Soviet aggression, and if need be against targets in the Soviet Union. The primary political purpose of the controversial deployment of United States GLCMs and Pershing II missiles in West Europe from 1983, at the request of West European governments, was to bring the Soviet Union within range of accurate US nuclear missiles based on the European continent, and to cement the United States' nuclear commitment in an era of superpower strategic parity at intercontinental level. Furthermore, the Soviet Union insists that it will retaliate against the American homeland if United States nuclear missiles strike the Soviet homeland, regardless of the launch-point of the missiles.

Even if the political and strategic factors considered above were conducive to the conduct of a superpower limited nuclear war in Europe (excluding European Russia), is such a scenario technically feasible? The technical difficulties in waging limited nuclear war at strategic, theatre or battlefield level are manifold. The most crucial is that of command, control and communications in a novel and extremely hostile nuclear environment.[13] For both superpowers the vulnerability of command, control and communications headquarters and facilities throughout the alliance blocs is relatively very high. In Soviet military doctrine counter-force attacks include strikes against United States command, control and communication facilities, and only a fraction of Soviet warheads would be required for such a task. Likewise only a fraction of the available United States warheads would be required to disable the Soviet facilities. It is United States policy in the early phases of a nuclear war not to target the Soviet leadership, and to induce some exercise of Soviet control, and,one would hope, deliberate restraint. However, even given good intentions on both sides, such would be the unprecedented level of damage, atmospheric disturbance impeding electronic communications, and stress on leadership with casualties mounting into the tens of millions, that there is reason to suspect that expectations of cohesive command and control of nuclear war, and the maintenance of communication facilities beyond the early nuclear exchanges, are not realistic:

> A strategic nuclear war between the United States and the Soviet Union would involve so many novel technical and emotional variables that predictions about its course – and especially about whether or not it can be controlled – must remain highly spectulative . . .
>
> Escalation is neither autonomous and inevitable nor subject completely to the decisions of any one national command authority. Whether or not it can be controlled will depend very much on the circumstances at the time. The use of a few nuclear weapons for some clear demonstrative purposes, for example, could well not lead to further escalation. However, it is most unrealistic to expect that there would be a relatively smooth and controlled progression from limited and selective strikes through major counterforce exchanges, to termination of the conflict at some level short of urban–industrial attacks. It is likely that beyond some relatively early stage in the conflict the strategic communications systems would suffer interference and disruption, the strikes would become ragged, uncoordinated, less precise and less discriminating and the ability to reach an agreed settlement between the adversaries would soon become extremely problematical.[14]

Wars rarely develop as planned or as anticipated: the First and Second World Wars stand as stark evidence of this. Following on the precedent of the Austro-Prussian War of 1866 and the Franco-Prussian War of 1870, it was expected that a war between the great powers in Europe in the early twentieth century would be over in the first two or three months, if not the first six weeks. It was reckoned that one or two decisive battles would determine the outcome of the war and, anyway, such were the interdependence and sensitivities of the economies of the great powers that a long war could not be sustained. In reality the opposite of all expectations was to occur. The general expectation of the Second World War was of a repeat of the land battles of attrition of the First World War, with the war being won by massive conventional bombing of civilians. The Second World War unfolded as a war of mass armies, but also a war of manoeuvre, often on a continental scale. In Europe, while massive conventional aerial bombing greatly assisted, final success required victory on the battlefield. In the Far East the use of the atomic bomb vindicated the role of the bomber as a war-winning instrument but, without the unique technological breakthrough of the atomic bomb, the Allied armies were faced with a long and bloody conquest of the home islands of the Japanese Empire.

Even in the limited or local wars of the international system since 1945, conflict has rarely followed the anticipated path. The Arab–Israeli wars, the wars in Korea and in south-east Asia, the current Iran–Iraq War in the Gulf have all displayed surprising and unexpected characteristics. Nuclear war is the greatest unknown, full of uncertainty, regardless of the plethora of sophisticated theories of limitation, and would probably develop in some unanticipated and horrific ways. At least in the context of conventional warfare there are some appropriate lessons to be drawn – cautiously. For nuclear war the only precedents are the atomic bombings of Hiroshima and Nagasaki in August 1945 by the crude, relatively low-yield atomic devices of the time. The imagery projected by those final acts of the Second World War is not reassuring when considering any breach of the nuclear threshold in a conflict between the superpowers in the European theatre.

Peace in the nuclear environment

Owing to the dangers and uncertainties of nuclear war, there has evolved in East–West relations a condition of 'nuclear peace', with its own unique characteristics. 'Waging peace' in a nuclear environment has produced aspects of state behaviour very different from that experienced before by the international system. There is a perpetual onus on military and civilian strategists and senior policy-makers to produce strategies and doctrines to keep the peace. This has been so in the West since the early 1950s, when the awesome implications of the development of nuclear power for military purposes began to be appreciated by the policy-making elites. Likewise, in the East, very soon after Stalin's death and after the Soviet Union's armed forces first acquired nuclear weapons, Malenkov was expressing doubts about the attraction of war in a nuclear world. His remarks were somewhat premature, and within two years he had lost his leading position in post-Stalin Soviet politics to the hawkish Khrushchev, who was backed by the military. But once secure in power, Khrushchev very quickly reversed his position, and a significant part of his de-Stalinization programme was to stress the importance of avoiding war with the West by pursuing foreign policy which would not promote military conflict.[15]

A major feature of Khrushchev's doctrine of peaceful coexistence, discussed at length in chapter 2, was that, owing to the increased strength of the socialist camp in the international system, war with the capitalist world need no longer be inevitable. The advance of socialism could be achieved without recourse to war. Traditionally, in international affairs, military matters assumed the highest priority just before or just after the outbreak of hostilities. When hostilities occurred military men were called upon to win the war. A glance at the relative unpreparedness for war of the democracies in West Europe in the late 1930s and in the United States in 1941 demonstrates this traditional approach to war. Governments and peoples, especially in the open societies of the international system, have always been reluctant to plan and procure for war until faced by the inevitability of conflict. There seems to have been some fear that to prepare for war could precipitate it. Given the memories of the First World War it is not surprising that this was the situation in West Europe in the 1930s. In the age before the development of mechanized armies and, later, nuclear missile arsenals, Britain and the United States could escape the worst consequences of unpreparedness. Before the advent of air power the maritime powers, graced by favourable geostrategic positions and with robust navies, could take some time to harness their demographic, industrial and military resources. For the continental European powers, except Russia by virtue of its unique geostrategic advantages, the advent of the steam and later the combustion engine removed the luxury of the gradual trans- formation of society from a state of peace to one of war. Now, in the age of nuclear missiles that can travel thousands of miles in a few minutes, and mass mechanized armies that may sweep across the European mainland in a matter of days, there is a state of perpetual military alert and preparedness. To be sure, there is also a state of peace, or 'non-war', in the developed world in the northern hemisphere, but this state of peace is very different from that understood and experienced before 1939.

As we are aware, in a nuclear world the superpowers and their respective alliance blocs in Europe want to achieve their foreign policy objectives and sustain their vital interests, but in the process *avoid* or, from the Soviet perspective, *prevent* war. In East–West relations in the past forty years there has been a persistent search for an alternative to war as an instrument to support objectives and protect interests. To date, in the West, for as long as a strategic doctrine has been officially enunciated, defence policies have been based on two strategic concepts derived from theories of deterrence – massive retaliation and flexible response. Central to both strategic concepts is the notion of the punishment of another state for transgression against the deterrer's interests. By the threat to exact costs, one state hopes to dissuade another from pursuing a particular policy:

> In its simplest form, deterrence can be seen as a particular type of social or political relationship in which one party tries to influence the behaviour of another in desired directions. Influence can, of course, be wielded in many different ways and for many different purposes. Deterrence, however, involves a particularly distinctive type of influ- ence that rests directly and openly upon threats of sanctions or deprivations. It is basically an attempt by party A to prevent party B from undertaking a course which A regards as undesirable, by threatening to inflict unacceptable costs on B in the event that the action is taken. Although this is a crude, rough and awkward definition, it nevertheless captures the essence of the concept. . .
>
> It is obvious from the definition that deterrence is an

attempt by party A to influence the intentions, and consequently the actual behaviour, of party B in a particular direction – that of inaction. Moreover, this attempt at exerting influence is very much a psychological phenomenon. It does not involve physically obstructing a certain course of action, but making that action appear costly and unattractive. Thus the strategy of deterrence attempts to influence B's perceptions or structure his image of the situation in such a way that he decides not to undertake the move he might have been contemplating. In other words, B is prevented from doing something by being made to believe that to refrain from the action is in his best interests. Deterrence, therefore, makes certain options or courses of action which are available to B, and possibly appear highly attractive and tempting, look most unattractive. Any potential gains to be made must be outweighed by the costs which B believes would be inflicted upon him in the event of a specified option being chosen or the prohibited action taken.[16]

Deterrence has always been attractive to the policy-making elites in the Western democracies with status quo objectives because, in the first instance, it forswears the prospect of war-fighting; and initially it played to Western strengths – a superiority in nuclear capabilities and in the high technology required to deliver the threat. The massive retaliation stance of John Foster Dulles during the Eisenhower administration was appealing precisely because it was seen to be cost-effective. There would be no need for large, expensive land armies, and resources could be devoted to the domestic economy. United States forces need not get bogged down again in dirty wars in faraway places such as Korea. The United States' defence was 'to depend primarily upon a great capacity to retaliate, instantly, by means and at places of our own choosing'.[17] The reality of massive retaliation was an awareness by the Eisenhower administration that there were limits to the deterrence effect of it nuclear weapons. In some conflict circumstances it would obviously be inappropriate and disproportionate to escalate nuclear war as a major act of retribution. Dulles himself made this clear in an article in *Foreign Affairs* in 1954:'Massive atomic and thermonuclear reaction is not the kind of power which could most usefully be evoked under all circumstances.'[18] At the same time, smaller, low-yield tactical nuclear weapons were coming into service in the United States armed forces. Nevertheless, throughout the Eisenhower period the distinct impression conveyed was of a crude but effective deterrence policy of retribution based upon US nuclear superiority.

Massive retaliation was not refined enough to constitute a war-fighting doctrine, but was meant to be perceived as the terrible price to be paid for breaking the ring of containment. It was not meant as an instrument to defeat the enemy in conflicts, on the ground, where they occurred. In its simplest interpretation, massive retaliation lacked considerable credibility; there were a number of political, ethical and strategic arguments which undermined any claim it could have had as a complete deterrence strategy. Its most important effect was to create considerable uncertainty in the minds of perceived adversaries as to what a United States response to open aggression might indeed be. There was the prospect, given the capabilities of the United States, that the response might be the worst. By the late 1950s the last vestiges of credibility of the declaratory policy of massive retaliation were disappearing. Strategic and technological developments, discussed in chapter 2, necessitated a rethink of nuclear doctrine in the United States. This, of course, given the leading role of the United States in the NATO Alliance, had great implications for West European defence and thinking about strategic doctrine.

The outcome of the strategic debate in the United States was the election of President Kennedy and the pronunciation and implementation of a new deterrence doctrine – the doctrine commonly known as flexible response, which is with us to this day. Flexible response covers the conventional through to nuclear deterrence spectrum, and the deterrence threat is inherent in the certainty of response. The notion is that aggression will be met with an appropriate level of force, and if this is found to be inadequate then escalation of force will take place:

A flexible response strategy assumes that NATO would try to convince the Soviets that the alliance would respond to any attack but that its response might initially be conventional, reserving the right to use nuclear weapons. NATO in fact seems to intend to respond to some kinds of conventional attack by conventional means. This strategy assumes that the deterrent, insofar as it depends on military force at all, depends primarily on convincing the Soviets that there will be a NATO response, including an American response. Deterrence depends much less on the form of military response than it does on the certainty of a response. Therefore, a certain conventional response to conventional aggression is a more credible tactical deterrent than the threat of a nuclear response.[19]

Massive retaliation, now more commonly known and measured as 'assured destruction', is at the end of the escalatory ladder which begins with a flexible response to initial aggression. The flexible response strategy is intended to give to Western policy-makers as many options as possible, at both conventional and nuclear, and tactical and strategic levels, in an effort to defend the status quo and threaten further costs if the enemy presses ahead. The ultimate sanction is counter-city strategic nuclear war. The concept of intra-war deterrence or graduated deterrence has created some ambiguity in the minds of many observers as to whether or not flexible response remains a deterrence strategy of retribution. Assured destruction has always been the ultimate punishment, but many of the increasingly sophisticated war-fighting options of the escalatory ladder appear to function less as a deterrent and more as an instrument of policy in the traditional Clausewitzian sense – that is, a move from deterrence to compellance. On the other hand, it could be argued that the distinction between retributive deterrence and the imposition of heavy costs through denial of victory on the battlefield is becoming increasingly blurred. What is certain is that, given the vulnerability of the American homeland from the 1960s and the rapid growth in the Soviet nuclear arsenal, the United States in particular can no longer posit a crude deterrence threat as a credible strategy for the defence of the Western Alliance.

For any threat of response to be credible and certain, a range of capabilities apposite to likely challenges at conventional and nuclear levels had to be procured, and a range of strategic options presented to decision-makers. There is considerable unhappiness in the West over the imperfections of Western deterrent strategy but over the past twenty-five years there has been a consensus in the West that deterrence by the threat of a certain response, perhaps leading to major, extremely costly retribution, is preferable to a traditional defensive posture which seems to tempt an adversary to settle issues of contention on the battlefield. Even successive French governments from de Gaulle onwards, which have frequently chosen not to fall into line with Washington's strategic concepts, have recognized the value of deterrence for national defence. Regardless of some moves in recent years to give French decision-makers some flexible options, French deterrence doctrine for the defence of the homeland is more akin to John Foster Dulles' massive retaliation than to the flexible response aspirations of Robert McNamara and subsequent United States secretaries of defence. Where deterrence breaks down, war fighting begins, and deterrence starts again, is a conceptual and practical problem difficult to define exactly. But given a commitment to protect deeply held values, is there any realistic alternative in the nuclear age? It could be argued that rather than actively implementing a deterrence strategy, the West finds itself in a deterrence condition, from which there is no credible avenue of escape.

Despite many assertions to the contrary, there has been a similar search in the East for the peaceful achievement of objectives and protection of interests. The Soviets do not accept Western concepts of deterrence. There is no equivalent Soviet word, and the terms used by the Soviets to correspond may be sderzhivanie, which means dissuasion or keeping out, or ustrashenie, which means intimidation. In recent years the former has been the word most widely used, yet neither really reflects what is understood by deterrence in the West.[20] The Soviets are frequently alarmed by what they perceive as the West's deterrence objectives. They are more inclined to ascribe the recent efforts to multiply deterrence options to a quest for war-fighting, perhaps first-strike capabilities, than to an attempt to enhance deterrence stability and overcome NATO's geos-trategic problems. The Russo-strategic perspective is that the technological advances in and doctrinal amendments to United States nuclear strategy in the 1970s attributed to Western deterrence a considerable power of compellance with offensive characteristics. While the United States was enunciating mutual assured destruction as the ultimate deterrent, it was making every effort to acquire war-fighting capabilities through which it could dominate and control any future nuclear conflict:

> Mutuality is further diminished by the fact that while the US spoke of 'mutual assured destruction' (MAD), in effect her policy was designed to increase counterforce capabili-ties – witness the MX missile programme, the *Trident* SLBM programme and improvement in forward-based systems (FBS) which simply amounted to 'outflanking' the SALT agreements. Even worse, PD-59 allegedly reflected the real intent of US policy, reinforced and supported by the release of previously secret US documents such as the operational plan Dropshot: US policy is designed to legitimise nuclear war by making the idea of limiting nuclear war more feasible and thus 'more acceptable', resulting in a lowering of the nuclear threshold, where a 'Euro-strategic nuclear war' might be pursued, leaving the USSR open to attack but giving sanctuary to the United States. Behind all this lies the intent of establishing (or re-establishing) escalation dominance and thus 'intimidat-ing' the USSR, or so the Soviet leadership reads the present situation.[21]

In the West much has been made of the reluctance of the Soviet military, in their professional journals, to accept the hopelessness of all-out war and the Western views of the role of retributive deterrence in war-avoidance. As outlined earlier, the Soviet military seem to insist that their role is to fight a future war, even nuclear, as they would fight any war, and defend the Soviet Union. Their objective seems to be to achieve victory (perhaps they mean 'survival'), [22] though there is an acute awareness in the Soviet military press of the catastrophic costs of any all-out war. In the event of the failure of 'deterrence', the

Soviet military see their role as fighting through the war, with conventional armies perhaps playing crucial roles in any post-nuclear phase of the conflict, rather than the military merely being the reflex instrument of punishment following an attack. However, the Soviet emphasis on defence in a classical manner, and on attempting to fight a war, does not imply a proclivity to wage war. To appreciate this an examination of how the Soviets view sderzhivanie, or what in the West would be described as Soviet deterrence doctrine, is required.

In the Soviet Union deterrence is perceived as a political instrument that is the responsibility of the political leadership. The Soviet leadership since Khrushchev has attached the highest priority to *preventing* a war between the West and the Soviet Union, by presenting before the West such aggregate power that war may not be viewed as a cost-effective option. Such Soviet power is composed not only of military might, but also of political influence, economic capabilities and social forces. As Khrushchev said at the 20th Congress of the CPSU in February 1956, 'Today there are mighty social and political forces possessing formidable means to prevent the imperialists from unleashing war, and if they actually try to start it, to give a smashing rebuff to the aggressors and frustrate their adventurist plans.'[23] The Soviet leadership since Khrushchev has viewed deterrence as a political doctrine composed of a whole range of forces and with a strength derived from the expansion since 1945 of the world Communist camp. Given the inherent political conflict between East and West, the Soviet leadership has always recognized war as a distinct and major danger, and acknowledged that it is the purpose of Soviet foreign policy to control political policy so as to prevent war.

The military instrument is a major instrument of foreign policy, but it is just one of the principal elements of deterrence policy for Moscow. 'In Soviet eyes, the prevention of war is not only a matter of the balance of military power, important though that is, but the object of a wider policy that embraces political elements as well.'[24] The Soviet military see their task as preparing to do their best, in the event of a failure of Soviet political policy, to defend the socialist camp, and if possible to be in a position to influence the postwar settlement. To the Soviet

Union the first line of defence is deterrence by the clear ability to deny your enemy gains, in contrast to the classical Western view of deterrence, which threatens punishment for attempting, or succeeding in making, gains.[25] In Soviet eyes military preparedness is seen to enhance war-prevention rather than weaken it:

> It is therefore mistaken to draw, as some commentators have done, a sharp contrast between the war-fighting policy of the Soviet Union and the war-deterring policy of the United States. The primary goal of Soviet military preparations is to prevent world nuclear war. At the same time, however, a strong emphasis on the need to prepare to wage such a war has been a distinctive feature of Soviet military thinking in the nuclear age.[26]

Although the major features of their deterrent doctrines differ in these respects, it is clear that both the United States and the Soviet Union wish to conduct their political competition and discourse without resort to nuclear war, and that they look to their own concepts of deterrence as a first line of defence. For both the nuclear superpowers and their alliance blocs, deterrence is very much an instrument of the nuclear peace in Europe, and while political postures may be modified and military aspects of deterrence changed to reflect technological and strategic developments, neither superpower has disowned the doctrines of deterrence that they have been practising since the mid-1950s. Indeed, as suggested above when discussing Western deterrence, it could be argued that it is a question of US deterrence doctrine inching towards the Soviet practice rather than, as has often been proposed, of the United States having revealed the magic of deterrence to the strategically unsophisticated Soviets in the course of arms control talks in the 1970s.

The strategic concept of deterrence has come under scrutiny and attack by a number of non-governmental groups in the West – sometimes with good cause. There are legitimate fears about the credibility of deterrence by retribution, if this means a major, perhaps devastating, response by the adversary. However, it is often overlooked that the initial action has to come from the adversary: it is the adversary who must determine the credibility of the deterrer's threat. Even if the credibility of any given response to aggression may seem low to some elements in the society of the deterrer, to the adversary the risks may be unacceptably high. There are genuine fears about the control of intra-war deterrence and the manageability of the controlled ascent of the ladder of escalation. There are also widespread qualms about the ethics and the morality of deterrence over and above the traditional aversion to the grim reality of the battlefield, given that the implementation of any threat could well result in disproportionate military responses and millions of non-combatant deaths. One may, or may not, fear or deride the imperfect strategic concept of deterrence, but *at least* it has not caused any East–West wars to date, and *at best* it may have prevented East–West conflict. A mere glance at the memoirs, papers and public statements of the major Eastern and Western statesmen of the past forty years – Eisenhower, Khrushchev, Macmillan, Kennedy, Brandt, Schmidt, de Gaulle, Heath, Brezhnev, Nixon – clearly demonstrates a caution and a prudence in their behaviour and pronouncements derived from an acute awareness of the deterrent effect of nuclear weapons.

This does not mean that complacency over the East–West deterrent balance should be encouraged. Unfortunately, in a world of intense political conflict, no statesmen, strategist or pressure group has offered a credible, practical alternative to deterrence. What should be encouraged is constant attention to the deterrence relationship between East and West. Attempts should be made constantly to sustain the East–West deterrent balance and, as far as possible, correct or manage any imperfections in it; but it is imperative that any modifications to the deterrence relationship should not be destabilizing. In the United States the early extravagant claims of some SDI enthusiasts in the Reagan administration that BMD could replace deterrence and all its imperfections with traditional defence have been modified fairly quickly. Administration spokesmen now suggest that BMD, if feasible in some form, could act as an adjunct to mutual deterrence, reducing some of the perceived vulnerabilities and weaknesses of the current superpower deterrence relationship – for instance, enhancing the survivability of the US land-based ICBM force. Whether or not this would enhance mutual deterrence if the Soviet land-based

ICBM force did not also have effective BMD is a moot question. Soviet land-based ICBMs constitute a much higher proportion of the country's strategic deterrent than does the land-based ICBM force of the United States' strategic deterrent, and 'the Soviet Union may (as it says it does) see American ABM R&D [research and development] as evidence of an attempt to deprive it of an effective retaliatory capability.'[27]

Competent deterrence, and a stable deterrence relationship between the superpowers, demands a constant attention to capabilities in order to sustain the credibility of the deterrer's threat. Competent deterrence requires that the deterrer has the weaponry to guarantee a retaliatory strike or, from the Soviet perspective, to wage war after a surprise attack. Ideally, both sides have the systems they identify as necessary for credible deterrence without undermining the deterrent credibility of the adversary. In other words, a situation of stable mutual deterrence is desirable, and has been the primary target of strategic arms control talks over the past fifteen years. In pursuit of this objective East–West arms control agreements, and the intellectual environment created by the arms control process, have been, in the short term, relatively successful. In the mid-1980s there is a mutual deterrence relationship between East and West, particularly in the northern hemisphere, where vital interests are clearly demarcated. But military high technology and research and development move at a great pace and at considerable expense. Constant attention to arms control and persistent evaluation of capabilities are essential. Mutual deterrence may require the unilateral introduction of new weapons systems, given some technological advances or increases in numbers by the adversary. On other occasions reductions in systems may be advisable and practised, given the political will, by arms controllers and governments. Unfortunately, with a few exceptions, the trend in the nuclear environment has been to build and deploy newer systems rather than to remove whole categories of systems from the bloc arsenals. When numbers are reduced it is usually because of obsolescence; or a few systems may be phased out in the glare of publicity for propaganda purposes. Recent instances of these unilateral initiatives are the 'Brezhnev offer', a reduction of twenty thousand Soviet troops and some tanks in

East Germany in 1980, and the Montebello decision of NATO in 1983. But the Soviet forces from East Germany were merely moved elsewhere in East Europe, and the fourteen hundred (out of six thousand) battlefield nuclear warheads removed by NATO had been seen to be old and redundant for many years.

Sustaining mutual deterrence in peacetime usually means modernizing nuclear arsenals, which may mean more launchers or more warheads, or upgrading command, control or communications facilities, or refining targeting planning. In peacetime, this induces among some observers a sense of foreboding, perhaps paranoia, as well as feelings of insecurity. This school of thought sees arms build-ups, whether in quantitative or qualitative terms, as contributing to if not creating political hostility which will inevitably lead to war. It is argued that what is perceived as military competition – arms races – between rival states creates a 'war psychology',[28] which will spontaneously burst into conflict at some critical point. But not everyone concurs with such perceptions:

> To attribute wars to arms is to confuse cause and effect. An arms race does not obey a logic of its own. It cannot be seen as an autonomous process divorced from the political context in which it occurs. Capabilities cannot be artificially separated from intentions. Military power serves the political ends of the state. An arms race reflects political tensions between nations; it does not cause these tensions. Armaments are needed by states to protect what they consider to be their interests. Nations do not fight because they possess arms. Rather, they possess arms because they believe it might some day be necessary to fight. Indeed, it can be shown that, when nations involved in political quarrels fail to arm themselves, they invite aggression. While it is true that when power confronts power there may be danger, it is certain that when power meets weakness there will be far greater danger. It is all too easy to point to conflicts and attribute them to arms races. It is much more difficult to point to wars which were prevented because nations guarded themselves.[29]

Most official opinion in the West adopts the latter perspective on the arms race, and so long as an acceptable degree of equivalence and parity in arsenals is sustained it produces stability in the central strategic balance and feelings of security. Over the past twenty years the foreign policy elites in the West and in the East have looked to arms control as an instrument to manage the inherent momentum of the arms race and sustain mutual deterrence. Each sustains their own suspicions of the motives of the other – which could well be misperceptions – but none the less, until the recent enthusiasm of the Reagan administration for ballistic missile defence, each has clearly recognized that a situation of mutual deterrence is to the mutual advantage of the superpower blocs.[30]

The arms control path is not always smooth, and is becoming increasingly complex, politically, technologically and strategically. But there has been success in the recent past, mutual deterrence has been sustained, and security for both East and West has been enhanced. For instance, to date both the United States and the Soviet Union have abided by the major terms of the SALT II Treaty, even though it was never ratified by the United States Congress, and Ronald Reagan, as a presidential candidate, declared his disapproval of it. Every effort must be made to perpetuate the arms control process. Arms races between the nuclear blocs may be inevitable for a plethora of reasons rooted both in the dynamics of internal and bureaucratic politics in East and West and in perceptions of external threats, but it is not beyond the capacity of man to control the competition and deliver an acceptable degree of security for both sides. In addition to the direct security requirement for arms control rather than unrestrained qualitative and quantitative arms competition, there is legitimate concern over the cost of arms competition. Over 500 billion dollars is being spent every year on arms in the world. The amount of aid given by the developed world to the underdeveloped world is but 5 per cent of the total used for military purposes. Apart from the ethical implications of such figures, such neglect of the underdeveloped world poses a whole range of long-term security questions. Within the societies of the superpowers the direct drain on resources caused by the expensive procurement of advanced military equipment is an increasingly acute burden. Both the

United States and the Soviet Union are aware of the real opportunity cost of unrestrained arms competition.

As we have seen, since 1945 East–West relations have been characterized more by prudent and cautious diplomacy than by irresponsible or miscalculated risk-taking. This has been particularly so in the European theatre, and there are few convincing arguments as to why this should not continue to be so. When major crises have developed in the European theatre, or on its periphery, but with security severely at risk in Europe, then prudence has been the order of the day. Nuclear threats have been used sparingly, and have been effective only in circumstances where there has been little doubt as to the value the superpower attaches to its interests and to the credibility of the threatened use of the military instrument. In this regard, on a relatively recent occasion, nuclear weapons performed a vital crisis management function.

Between 24 and 26 October 1973, during the Yom Kippur War in the Middle East, a superpower confrontation arose with acute nuclear dimensions. Israel broke a UN sponsored ceasefire, and in the course of a successful counter-offensive into African Egypt surrounded the Egyptian Third Army at Suez. Faced by the imminent collapse of its major Middle Eastern 'client', Moscow proposed to Washington a joint US–Soviet peace-keeping force. Washington immediately rejected such a notion. The Nixon administration did not want a major Soviet military presence in the Middle East. It did not want to present the image of superpower condominium to the international system, in particular to the West Europeans, and wanted the postwar diplomatic situation to be as fluid and flexible as possible – which would not be the case with a major Soviet presence. In the face of the United States' refusal, the Soviet Union threatened unilateral action and proposed to do the job themselves; ostentatious military moves were made to demonstrate their intention. The United States' response, in the early morning hours of 25 October, was to declare DEFCON (Defence Readiness Condition) III for all US forces worldwide. Parts of Strategic Air Command (SAC) and the Polaris and Poseidon fleets are regularly kept in DEFCON III, but all other forces were moved up one state of readiness. In particular the world's attention was drawn to the increased readiness of all US nuclear forces, though, of course, the alert applied to conventional forces as well: for example, the 82nd Airborne Division began to embark. Indeed, DEFCON III was not a threat

> to unleash nuclear war, but to get involved in a situation militarily and to pursue an escalating process despite awareness that its potential consequences were incalculable. The nuclear threat, in short, served to make clear just how importantly the United States viewed the stakes in the situation and the ultimate cost which could be suffered by the Soviet Union if it initiated a process of military interaction.[31]

The Soviet Union quickly backtracked on its unilateral moves. The shock of the United States' alert stabilized the crisis and the military situation on the Egyptian–Israeli front. The historic American interest in the region, the power-projection capabilities, and the will of the Nixon administration to keep the Soviets militarily out of that vital strategic part of the world, were all clearly demonstrated. There could be no doubt that the United States was willing to go to war to safeguard its interests. It also shocked the Israelis into caution, illustrated to Cairo that the US did not see the fall of Sadat as being in its interests, and reassured the dispirited West Europeans that the Gaullist spectre of superpower condominium over Europe and its environs was not going to emerge from the Middle East. Initially some commentators thought the DEFCON III an over-reaction to the crisis. But given the fog of war in the Middle East, the domestic political fog in the United States created by the tortuous progress of the Watergate scandal, and the confusion and suspicion within the Atlantic Alliance exacerbated by the use of the Arab oil against the vulnerable West European economies, a lucid and unequivocal signal of intent and commitment was required.

Another major characteristic of the nuclear peace has been the evolution of the rival alliance systems in Europe – political–military blocs of considerable longevity and geopolitical scope. The Warsaw Pact has survived for over thirty years, and NATO for over thirty-five. This is surprising given the propensity of alliances in modern history to dissolve after only a few years, and to be exceedingly brittle the more members they encompass and the greater their geopolitical scope. NATO now has sixteen members, and borders the Black Sea and Barents Sea in the East and the Pacific in the West. For an alliance of such geographical scope and political diversity to have sustained its cohesion over such a long period is an historical phenomenon. Constant public attention is paid to the periodic crises which erupt within NATO over such issues as nuclear weapons strategy or burden-sharing. Yet there are elemental forces of considerable strength, usually overlooked and taken for granted, that have sustained the integrity of NATO. This is all the more remarkable given that NATO, in stark contrast to the Warsaw Pact, is a voluntary association of sovereign states. There can be little doubt that not only do governments but also the publics of the NATO members perceive the worth of the North Atlantic Alliance, in spite of its much publicized internal arguments and shortcomings. The major cohesive force in NATO remains the general perception that the Soviet Union and its allies pose serious threats to the political integrity of the member states of the North Atlantic Alliance, and that the Alliance does present a credible deterrent to war while sustaining the peace. In the past thirty-five years, governments which support the Alliance have consistently been returned to office throughout West Europe and North America. Political parties which are seen to waver or equivocate risk grave electoral consequences and invariably pay the price. It may be a misperception, but it seems that throughout the West there is a general consensus that NATO is an essential pillar of the nuclear peace, and that war would be more likely if the Alliance was to disintegrate.

A consequence of the foundation of NATO, and its growth to incorporate West Germany, was the formalization of the Soviet Union's defence arrangements in East Europe in a multilateral alliance system in 1955. It is clear from events in East Europe since 1955 that the Warsaw Pact is not a voluntary alliance in the same sense as NATO. Hungary attempted to leave in 1956 and was prevented from doing so in a most bloody manner. The prospect of Czechoslovakia breaking the political conformity of the Pact was one motive behind the military intervention by neighbouring Communist states led by the Soviet Union in 1968.

In most East European states the Soviet Union sustains military forces of a strength exceeding that required by defence only. For instance, in the German Democratic Republic there are twenty Soviet divisions, in Czechoslovakia there are five, and in Hungary there are four. Such forces obviously fulfil an occupation as well as a defence role. Yet for the Communist regimes in power in East Europe, though certainly not for many of the people, such roles for the Soviet military forces are not all that distinct from defence. These are regimes that perceive themselves as existing in a hostile international environment in which class conflict is endemic and does not stop at the frontiers of, for instance, the German Democratic Republic or Hungary. They fear hostile elements within their own society as much if not more than a thrust by a resurgent West Germany into the old battlefield of East Europe or the unleashing of the United States' war machine in a gigantic effort to eradicate Communism.

Whatever the perceptions and motives of the state actors on either side of the Iron Curtain – and it should be remembered that within both alliances there are differing degrees and types of commitment to the blocs by the member states – the political and ideological demarcation of Europe is clear; there are no political 'grey areas' remaining in Europe. Both alliance blocs are well aware of the value the other places on every inch of European territory. Even the position of the neutral states is unambiguous. For instance, in Scandinavia a clear 'Nordic pattern' or 'balance' of security has developed, the political configuration of which both alliance blocs respect and support.[32] There is no doubt in Moscow that any Soviet attack on Sweden would be unacceptable to NATO and would at the very least plunge East–West relations to depths never experienced even in the darkest days of the Cold War, and would probably result in war. Likewise, in Western capitals there is an acute appreciation of the unique geostrategic importance of Finland to the Soviet Union, and it would undermine the whole Scandinavian security edifice, if not endanger all of Europe, to attempt to woo Helsinki from its special relationship with Moscow. In the case of Austria, neutrality was a precondition for the Soviet Union to agree to the withdrawal of the occupying powers in 1955. Austrian neutrality is legal neutrality, incorporated into the Austrian State Treaty of

1955 and guaranteed by the former occupying powers. If Austria were ever to propose joining an alliance then any of the former occupying powers would be legally entitled to intervene with military force and reoccupy the country. Alliances are especially useful in defining strategic frontiers in sensitive, competitive areas, and in that regard it could be advanced that NATO and the Warsaw Pact are a boon to security and stability in contemporary Europe.

4

Geopolitical Accommodation

For more than thirty years there has been no significant geopolitical realignment in Europe. Buttressed and constrained by the imperatives of ideological conformity and the balance of nuclear power, territorial boundaries have not been altered, nor has the ideological allegiance of governments or regimes on either side of the Iron Curtain changed. The division of labour agreed at Yalta, the *de facto* boundaries which emerged at Potsdam, and the political arrangements for the administration of Germany and East Europe which developed from East–West competition in Europe from 1945 up to the foundation of the East and West German states in 1949, have ossified. While there has been some political accommodation to European geopolitical realities in recent years, there has been little actual change in the geopolitical configuration of European politics since 1949. There have been no major retreats or advances for the East or the West in Europe, and the Iron Curtain remains where it was in 1949.

In 1961 Albania, a signatory of the Warsaw Treaty of 1955, announced that it was ceasing to be an active member. The ultra-orthodox regime in Tirana chose to align with Peking rather than Moscow in the growing Sino-Soviet split. Isolated as Albania is from the rest of the Warsaw Pact by Yugoslavia and Greece on its land borders, and with a coastline on the Adriatic facing west towards Italy, effective political or military pressure could not be brought to bear on the country by the Soviet Union. Albania was never expelled from the Warsaw Pact, and did not formally withdraw until September 1968 in protest over the Pact invasion of Czechoslovakia the previous month. While the defection of Albania could be viewed as a 'loss' for Soviet Communism in Europe, it most certainly was not a gain for the West. Albania has, in isolation, continued along an idiosyncratic, autarkic, Stalinist path, and Peking has made little use of its political bridgehead in Europe. Because of Albania's geographical position and minimal political and economic importance, its defection has had no significant effect on European security.

Elsewhere in East Europe major initiatives to implement change have been ruthlessly crushed. In Budapest in 1956 and in Prague in 1968 (with the assistance of other East European allies) the Red Army enforced the geopolitical status quo. Hungary was not allowed to leave the Warsaw Pact and the Dubcek government in Czechoslovakia was prevented from pursuing its policy of liberalizing Czechoslovakian socialism. The emergence of the Solidarity free trade union in Poland in 1980 posed a severe challenge to the political authority of the Communist Party in Poland. By late 1981 Solidarity was making clear political as well as economic demands, and raising the prospect of a pluralist political structure in Poland.[1] At the Solidarity Congress in September and October 1981, 'demands included a call for free elections, economic self-management, free access to media, and final legalisation of free labour unions.'[2]

The democratization and liberalization of Poland in 1980 and 1981 created considerable anxiety in the other Warsaw Pact regimes, particularly in Poland's neighbours to the east and to the west – the Soviet Union and the German Democratic Republic. By late 1981 the activities and successes of Solidarity seemed to combine the threats posed to ideological conformity in East Europe by the mass popular support for the Hungarian uprising, and the progressive politics of the Dubcek experience in Czechoslovakia. Soviet and Warsaw Pact concern was expressed through extensive military manoeuvres in March and April 1981, code-named Soyuz 81, under the direct command of Marshal Kulikov, Soviet Commander of the Warsaw Pact forces. 'During the manoeuvres the Soviet, East German and Czechoslovakian Warsaw Pact forces simulated a landing on the Polish coast and a surprise night attack.'[3] Given the probability of some severe opposition if there should be direct military intervention by the Red Army, Moscow was reluctant to use the military instrument directly to secure the position of the Communist Party as it had done in Hungary and Czechoslovakia. Under some pressure from Moscow, General Jaruzelski, the Polish Prime Minister since October 1981, used Polish forces, primarily specially trained internal security units, to restore the political authority of the demoralized Communist Party in December of the same year. More than 6,000 opposition activists were arrested, and many of the concessions which Solidarity had wrung from the government were removed. The Jaruzelski coup re-established the monopoly of political and economic policy-making in the party without the necessity of military intervention by other Warsaw Pact armies. One suspects that without Jaruzelski's firm action a Soviet-led military intervention and a bloody struggle would have been inevitable, in order to sustain ideological conformity throughout the Warsaw Pact. A repetition of Hungary 1956 was avoided, but in the short term the political outcome seems to have been the same.

The appeal of the Soviet model of Communism in the West has not been such as to spark spontaneous enthusiasm, political revolution or the advance of the Iron Curtain any further west than the limit it reached with the fall of Czechoslovakia into the Soviet camp in 1948. Nor has the vigour and dynamism of capitalism been such that the inefficient and brittle Communist systems in East Europe have been cowed or have lost vital territory since the defection of Yugoslavia to non-alignment in June 1948. Yugoslavia, a state which has pursued its own unique brand of Communism and its own robust non-alignment, was not liberated by the Red Army. Tito's own partisan army liberated large parts of Yugoslav territory before the collapse of the German occupation. As a result there was not only a sense of independence, but also the reality. The inability of Moscow to sustain practical control over Tito in 1948 was a demonstration of the real limits of Stalin's military and political reach, under-appreciated by the West at the time.

Since the lifting of the Berlin blockade in 1949 there have been two significant geopolitical developments which *regularized* the division of Europe between hostile blocs, rather than leading to or heralding the dissolution of the prevailing security arrangements. On 15 May 1955 the Austrian State Treaty was signed, which permanently neutralized the state of Austria and led to the withdrawal of the Western and Soviet occupying forces from their respective zones. Unlike the Soviet zone in Germany, no Communist state had been established there, so it would be a mistake to see the Austrian State Treaty as a political or ideological retreat on the part of the Soviet Union. At the time, Soviet agreement to the treaty came as a surprise, but the general view is that the geopolitical and strategic advantages for Moscow far outweighed the 'loss' of some territory. Moscow may have intended the treaty to reveal to the Federal Republic the advantages of neutral status, and simultaneously to elevate the status of the Soviet Union in the eyes of the growing non-aligned movement in the decolonizing world outside Europe.

In 1955 the Federal Republic entered NATO, but the neutralization of Austria broke continuous Western lines of communication between the Federal Republic and Italy; with Switzerland to the west, Austria split NATO in half between north and south. In the run-up to the Geneva summit of July 1955, the Austrian State Treaty was good public relations for Moscow and for the emerging leader, Nikita Khrushchev, who was enthusiastic to make his mark on the world stage and establish a rapport with Eisenhower. The neutralization of Austria removed British occupying forces from the southern zone of the country where it bordered on Yugoslavia and Hungary, while also reducing the overt threat to Tito's position from Soviet forces to the north of Yugoslavia. One of Khrushchev's major foreign policy objectives in 1955 was to re-establish cordial relations with Tito's Yugoslavia, following the bitter political hostility of the last five years of Stalin's rule and the intense propaganda barrage suffered by Yugoslavia from the Sino-Soviet bloc. Yugoslavia demonstrated to the rest of East Europe that a state could be Communist and nationalist and survive, without integration into the Soviet East European glacis. Khrushchev and Bulganin visited Belgrade eleven days after the signing of the Austrian State Treaty: relations on a state-to-state basis between Yugoslavia and the Soviet Union improved, but no situation of trust between Tito and the Communist party leadership in Moscow ever developed.

Yugoslavia has persisted in its independent, non-aligned policy, and Tito never accepted any invitations to visit Moscow.

The second development was the construction of the Berlin wall, which began with the erection of wire fences on 13 August 1961. Within a few days there were only four crossing-points on the thirty-mile boundary between East and West Berlin. All essential areas of control in the Soviet zone of Berlin – East Berlin – were handed over to the German Democratic Republic. In the three years of the Berlin crisis of 1958–61 refugees poured into West Berlin from the GDR, depleting the East German economy of some of its most skilled labour and causing severe political embarrassment for the regime. The Berlin crises had been provoked by the Soviet Union, in an attempt to bolster the legitimacy of the German Democratic Republic by obliging the occupying powers in the Western zones of the city to deal with the East German government over access to Berlin across East German territory. Khrushchev also suggested that West Berlin should become a 'free' city, demilitarized and independent. The Soviet Union was making a major effort to remove the anomaly of a capitalist enclave inside East Europe, and to strengthen its policy of a distinctly divided Germany. The Western allies had compelling political and strategic reasons to sustain their foothold in West Berlin. Success for Khrushchev would have

undermined the Four Powers' responsibility for all-German affairs and severed the tenuous political–constitutional link between West Berlin and West Germany. As reflected in the special provisions made for West Berlin in West Germany's constitution, the Western powers had never been enthusiastic about too specific and visible an integration of West Berlin into the Federal Republic, primarily because they wanted to preserve the legal claim that West Berlin was under the authority of the occupying powers. Although there was a *de jure* separation between West Berlin and the Federal Republic, there was a *de facto* economic, political and symbolic connection that was as strong as that between East Berlin and East Germany – a connection that Bonn was determined to maintain. The creation of an isolated miniature state of West Berlin would have shut out the Western powers by abolishing the Four Power Agreement, and it would have excluded the political influence of the Federal Republic. A major political ambiguity standing in the way of the Soviet two-Germanies policy would have been clarified and resolved in Moscow's favour.[4]

If the Western allies had compromised on West Berlin, then Bonn's confidence in the commitment of NATO to safeguarding the Federal Republic's vital interests would have declined. A likely consequence could have been the collapse of NATO, following a withdrawal of the Federal Republic and perhaps accommodation by Bonn with the East. But by 1961, a foreign policy designed to support the existence of the GDR began to threaten its survival. The Berlin wall stopped the *Menschenraub* (literally, the people theft)[5] and cemented not only the division of Berlin, but also the division of Germany. In theory, Berlin was *one* city, jointly administered by four occupying powers as agreed at Yalta. Under the Four Power Agreement there was no legal right to build the wall but, as the Western zones in the city were left secure, the Western allies were not prepared to force the issue. The Berlin wall did not change any territorial boundaries or political allegiances. It regularized the *de facto* territorial and political reality of Berlin, and removed the political arrangements for the city as a major item of crisis on the East–West agenda. The Western allies were not denied access to East Berlin, but were restricted to specific crossing points. Indeed, in many quarters the wall was greeted with a sense of relief. It brought the crisis to a conclusion, but not in the manner initially threatened by the Soviet Union. A separate peace treaty between the German Democratic Republic and the Soviet Union was not concluded, the position of the Western allies in West Berlin was not called into question, and the access routes to the city from the West were not put in jeopardy – all of which could have led to open conflict. As Willy Brandt has commented, 'What we in Berlin regarded as a cruel blow may almost have come as a relief to others.'[6] Perhaps most important of all, the wall demonstrated that, in an effort to achieve re-unification on the West's terms, the hard-line foreign policy of the Adenauer administration towards the East had failed, and that in the long term a political accommodation was necessary.

Since the construction of the Berlin wall there has been some popular support for geopolitical change in Europe, in both the East and the West. In the East the 'Prague Spring' of 1968, the birth and rapid growth of the Polish Solidarity movement in 1980–81, and the blossoming of human rights and unofficial peace movements in many East European countries, all demonstrate a grass-roots impatience with the geopolitical status quo in Europe. This is not to suggest that such developments are coordinated or that there is any set of radical, coherent political objectives shared by these disparate groupings. Nor is it to suggest, apart from brief moments in Czechoslovakia in 1968 and in Poland in 1980 and 1981, that any severe threat has been posed to the political status quo within the East European countries of the Soviet bloc or to the integrity of the bloc itself. But what is proposed is that there may be many ordinary people, military men and Communist Party members who are dissatisfied with the present political–security arrangements of forty years' standing in East Europe, and long for greater economic and political freedom and national independence in foreign affairs. As described in chapter 1, there has been an upsurge of protest in West Europe in recent years, aimed primarily at the standing arrangements for European security and, in particular, at the presence and role of the superpowers and nuclear weapons. This has led to the radicalization of the foreign and defence policies of some of the major West European political parties, for instance the British Labour Party and the West German SPD, and the birth in West Germany of a new party dedicated to major changes in the defence field – the Green Party.

Nevertheless, in the past twenty years state governments and the alliances in Europe, in both the East and the West, have chosen not to attempt any radical change of the geopolitical status quo, but to accommodate inter-state relations across the Iron Curtain to geopolitical realities. Within and between governments, regardless of the ebb and flow of popular movements, there has been a consensus that accommodation between East and West is more conducive to European security and stability than risk-taking efforts to challenge the other bloc's vital interests in a sensitive, nuclear environment. Undoubtedly, actors in both East and West see accommodation as serving their own different, long-term, policy objectives. In the West, accommodation was chosen as the route to greater contact with the East, the breakdown of ideological barriers, and perhaps the long-distant eventual loosening of the Soviet grip on East Europe. In the East, accommodation has been seen as reinforcing the position of the Communist regimes in East Europe, especially the German Democratic Republic, and securing a universal acknowledgement of the pre-eminent role of the Soviet Union in East European affairs. The aspirations of the radical groups in East and West Europe have rarely been manifest in actual inter-state relations within the blocs or between them. The European *détente* of the late 1960s and the 1970s – Ostpolitik, the CSCE process and the arms control talks in Europe – has 'legitimized' the status quo, rather than making any short- to medium-term attempt to change it.

Ostpolitik

Following the construction of the Berlin wall, there was some uncertainty in the Federal Republic about what to do next. 'Should Bonn abandon the "maintained tensions" policy of Adenauer towards the East and do a deal, should Bonn wait, in a patient and relaxed manner, for the superpowers to come to some agreement, or should Bonn directly approach the German Democratic Republic?', was the question exercising those concerned with settling the German question and reducing tensions in central Europe. The Social Democratic Party, in opposition, demonstrated a willingness to support openings to the East, though, at that time, this was not quite as radical as the propositions of the philosopher Karl Jaspers which started a major public debate. Jaspers argued that West German policy ought to stop concentrating on the formalities of reunification and pay more heed to the welfare of German people in East Europe, especially in the German Democratic Republic.[7] Initially unpopular, Jaspers' arguments soon began to gather support. There was a growing awareness that with the changes in the international environment the context of the German question in East–West relations was being transformed. In the world of emerging *détente*, and with the attention of the superpowers and others turning to issues such as arms control, there was a danger that West German foreign policy could find itself out of step with the interests and concerns of its allies in the West as well as with its adversaries in the East.

Before leaving office in 1963 Adenauer was willing to countenance change, but it was the government of Erhard and Foreign Minister Schröder which initiated the 'policy of movement'. The general strategy was to apply pressure on the GDR by isolating it from its fellow East European states. The Hallstein Doctrine foreclosed the option of opening formal diplomatic relations with states which recognized the GDR, except for the Soviet Union. But it was felt that the attraction of economic links with the Federal Republic could lead to quasi-formal relations between Bonn and the GDR's neighbours. Trade missions were set up in Warsaw, Budapest, Sofia and Bucharest. The Hallstein Doctrine was abandoned in 1966, and in January 1967 formal relations were opened with Rumania, and then with Yugoslavia in early 1968. In August 1967 a trade mission was opened in Prague. Despite the extant West German territorial and political claims, which placed a major hurdle before any substantial improvement in West German–East European relations, the situation did improve among the East European states, except for the German Democratic Republic. Moscow looked askance at such developments, and only welcomed long-term agreements with the Federal Republic which would legitimize the GDR and put constraints on the prospect of the Federal Republic ever possessing nuclear weapons.

By the mid 1960s the GDR had become one of the leading economic powers in East Europe, and Moscow's loyalist ally, and it occupied the most important strategic position in the Warsaw Pact. The prospect of a successful outflanking diplomatic manoeuvre by the Federal Republic against the GDR alarmed Moscow and East Berlin, not only because of its effect on the GDR but also because of its deleterious effect on the Soviet grip on East Europe. The virtual abandonment of the policy of 'maintained tensions' and the Hallstein Doctrine, and public overtures of *rapprochement* with East Europe – such as a declaration by the Grand Coalition government of Kurt Kiesinger, whose Foreign Secretary was Willy Brandt, that the 1938 Munich Agreement was invalid and that reconciliation with Poland was desirable – did little to allay Soviet and East German anxieties. The result was implacable opposition and a call for Pact solidarity by the Soviet Union. Demands were made of the Federal Republic and the Western allies designed to disrupt the 'policy of movement'. The famous Bucharest Declaration of July 1966 by the Political Consultative Committee of the Warsaw Pact laid down:

> that the preconditions for a lasting peace in Europe were Bonn's recognition of the viability of the existing frontiers between European states and its renunciation of all territorial claims and interest in acquiring nuclear weapons. The principles of independence and non-intervention were emphasised. The strong denunciation of the Federal Republic was qualified by a provision stressing the importance of strengthening relations between these States regardless of their political systems. The Declaration also called for the abolition of military blocs and for other measures of military disengagement.[8]

At the April 1967 meeting of European Communist and workers' parties at Karlovy Vary in Czechoslovakia the declaration called for 'the West's acceptance of Europe's existing boundaries; the acknowledgement of the GDR's claims to full diplomatic recognition; invalidation of the Munich Agreement (diktat); renunciation of the Hallstein Doctrine; acceptance of West Berlin as a separate political entity; ratification of the NPT [Non-Proliferation Treaty]; and renunciation of the use of force.'[9]

The Soviet Union was particularly anxious about too close a *rapprochement* between the Federal Republic and Warsaw Pact countries of the strategically important 'northern tier'. By 1968 Czechoslovakia was a particular source of concern. Increasing economic contacts between Bonn and Prague, together with the liberalization process inside Czechoslovakia, raised fears in Moscow about the continued control of the Czechoslovakian

Communist Party. The distinct possibility that Prague, followed by Budapest, would open formal diplomatic relations with Bonn was a source of further alarm. In August 1968 Warsaw Pact forces invaded Czechoslovakia, ostensibly on the absurd pretext that supplies of NATO weapons had been infiltrated into Czechoslovakia to support a counter-revolutionary uprising.[10] Whatever the real reason for the invasion, the outcome of the episode for European security arrangements in the late 1960s was obvious:

> The Russians made clear that they would not permit a marked growth of economic and other ties between their allies and the FRG, or at least would require in exchange a high political price in the form of German confirmation of the status quo including the frontiers of central Europe and the hitherto unthinkable concession, recognition of the other German state.[11]

Faced with stalemate in relations with the East, or a new approach, some sections of opinion in Bonn, notable in Willy Brandt's SPD, realized that any new constructive relations between the Federal Republic and East Europe required Moscow's approval in the first instance. The Grand Coalition collapsed in 1969, and in October of that year a new SPD/FDP coalition, which was to survive until 1983, took power, determined to launch a new policy initiative towards the East, via Moscow rather than outflanking it. A price would have to be paid, but Brandt realized that there was little alternative. Despite the mere 'traffic accident' of the invasion of Czechoslovakia, as de Gaulle's Foreign Minister Michel Debré described it, East–West *détente* was gathering pace. Superpower discussions on a European security conference, strategic arms limitation and the non-proliferation of nuclear weapons experienced only a temporary hiccup. Washington was advising Bonn that '*détente* with the East offered the best hope of solving Germany's problems.'[12] To turn its back on the East would be to leave the Federal Republic out of mainstream East–West *détente*, jeopardize United States–Federal Republic relations, and leave Bonn in splendid Cold War isolation in the North Atlantic Alliance, while the long-term

questions of the political future and military security of the two
Germanies and much of the rest of central and East Europe
would remain unresolved.

Willy Brandt entered office as Chancellor determined to avoid
the mistakes of the Ostpolitik of the Grand Coalition. He saw it
as essential to define the foreign policy objectives of the Federal
Republic towards the East more clearly than before, and to give a
clear signal that the SPD/FDP policy would differ from that
which preceded it. Moscow, Warsaw and East Berlin were to be
persuaded of the non-offensive nature of Brandt's Ostpolitik. An
illustration of this was the Federal Republic's self-denial of
nuclear weapons when it signed the Non-Proliferation Treaty a
month after Brandt took office. Brandt was aware of the Soviet
objective of formalizing the status quo in Europe, and saw that
this could be used to promote Bonn's interests – that is, to make
West Berlin more secure, to improve the human condition of
Germans throughout East Europe and to bring the two
Germanies closer together. Reunification and *détente* were seen to
be impossible bedfellows, so reunification, while not abandoned
as a goal, was avoided as a contemporary issue. The invasion of
Czechoslovakia in 1968 actually made the new Bonn government's task easier. The shock made it evident that a reorganization of European security arrangements was not feasible, and
that only a policy which included acknowledgement of the
geopolitical status quo was practicable.

A direct approach was required. Within a month of the
SPD/FDP coalition coming to power, West German–Soviet
discussions began on a non-aggression treaty. In August 1970 a
West German–Soviet treaty was signed, which accepted the
existing frontiers in Europe, including those between the two
Germanies. This was a major contribution towards the regularization of geopolitical conditions in central Europe. By implica-
tion, the actuality of a treaty between Moscow and Bonn
recognized the Federal Republic as a reliable state in the
international community, contrary to all Soviet and East
European propaganda between 1949 and 1970, and often since
1970. Bonn made it clear to Moscow that a reciprocal acknowledgement of the status quo in Berlin was required: ratification
by the Bundestag of the West German–Soviet treaty was to be

used as the lever to persuade Moscow in this direction. Indeed, the treaty was not ratified until the four powers in Berlin successfully concluded the Quadripartite Agreement regularizing issues such as West Berlin's status, access to West Berlin, and visiting rights to East Berlin and East Germany. This in turn was underwritten by an agreement on Berlin between the two Germanies.[13] The quadripartite discussions were taking place simultaneously with Brandt's discussions with Moscow and later with Warsaw. In September 1971 the Quadripartite Berlin Agreement was concluded, and in December of the same year the Inter-German Agreement on Berlin was initialled. With the Moscow and Warsaw treaties hanging in the balance, there was every incentive for the Soviet Union and Poland to put pressure on a somewhat unwilling GDR to accommodate the Federal Republic's and Western allies' wishes on Berlin. In May 1972 the Bundestag ratified the Moscow and Warsaw treaties, and a month later Moscow signed the Berlin Agreement.

A major hurdle in the Moscow Treaty had been an attempt by the GDR to make explicit legal recognition of the East Berlin regime an essential element of the agreement, but Bonn could not side-step its constitutional commitment to the long-term goal of reunification. Moscow gave way to Bonn on that issue. Nowhere in the treaty is the term 'recognition' actually used. The frontiers of all states are declared 'inviolable' but not unalterable within the context of the free consent of peoples. It was agreed that the Federal Republic would reach agreements with Poland, the GDR and Czechoslovakia, and that all of the West German Ostpolitik treaties 'would constitute an integrated whole'[14] which would contribute to European security. Most importantly, the use of force as a means to change frontiers was renounced. Also, Moscow accepted a 'letter on German unity' from Foreign Minister Scheel which stated that the objective of German reunification remained, but only in the context of free self-determination.[15]

While some East European states were uneasy that Moscow had not pressed for complete recognition of the territorial status quo, many in the West, including the Federal Republic, thought Moscow had got the better of the deal. A number of advantages for Moscow were identified. First was the formalization, even though it was not the legitimization, of the territorial status quo in central and East Europe. The emerging *détente* with the West which Moscow sought, not just on security grounds but also for reasons of economic and technological contact with the advanced economies of the West, would not be hampered by a recalcitrant Federal Republic. Some pessimists saw in the Moscow Treaty the roots of an attempt to draw the Federal Republic towards the East politically and economically and to create a fissure in the Atlantic Alliance. In February 1970 a commercial agreement was included whereby Soviet natural gas was delivered to the Federal Republic in return for West German credits of over one billion Deutschmarks to finance West German–Soviet trade.

In December 1970 a Federal Republic–Poland treaty quickly followed on the West German–Soviet treaty. The Warsaw Treaty confirmed the main elements of the Moscow Treaty, including the renunciation of force, the acknowledgement of existing frontiers including the Oder–Neisse line as Poland's western frontier, and an undertaking to set up relations with the GDR. The Poles pressed hard for formal recognition of the frontiers, but came to realize that this would make the treaty unratifiable in the West German Bundestag. As with the Moscow Treaty, there was no insistence by Warsaw that Bonn give the GDR full recognition. In the light of recent European history, the renunciation of force element was very important for the Polish government. Also, as with the Moscow Treaty, there was a parallel economic agreement. In October 1970, the Federal Republic and Poland signed a five year trade agreement which was the most generous ever for an East European country trading with the West. Amongst other things, Poland was granted an annual credit of 500 million Deutschmarks for five years, and Federal Republic trade restrictions were fully removed from 80 per cent of Polish imports (1,200 items) and relaxed on 4,000 additional items.[16] A humanitarian aspect of the Bonn–Warsaw *rapprochement* was a separate agreement, outside the formal treaty, for Poland to adopt a liberal view on ethnic Germans wishing to emigrate to West Germany to be reunited with their families. Also, Brandt's political initiative to the East was being supported by an underpinning of ever-expanding economic agreements with East European states eager for commercial links with the economic giant of West Europe. For instance, in October 1970 the Federal Republic and Hungary agreed to a long-term trade relationship. In 1970 total trade between Hungary and the Federal Republic amounted to 1,000 million Deutschmarks, a 40 per cent increase over 1969.[17]

The year 1970 also witnessed the opening of direct discussion between the two Germanies but the talks dragged on, with difficult phases, for nearly three years.[18] The German Democratic Republic, of course, ever fearful for its long-term sovereignty, was determined upon full recognition, which Bonn, while prepared to acknowledge the inner-German border (IGB) as an inviolable political–legal entity and the reality of the GDR as a functioning state, could not comply with. It would actually have been against the Federal Republic's Basic Law (constitution) to do so; to give full recognition to the GDR would have demanded a two-thirds vote of the Bundestag to amend the Basic Law, not a simple majority vote to ratify the treaty. Anyway, given four power responsibilities, Bonn and East Berlin could not by their own will legitimize the permanent division of Germany. East–West *détente*, the Moscow and Warsaw treaties of 1970, and the Quadripartite Agreement on Berlin in 1971, put the German Democratic Republic regime in an impossible position, obliging them eventually to sign the Basic treaty between the two Germanies in December 1972. The Basic Treaty was predicated on the notion of eventual reunification, but the extant autonomy and independence of the two German states – not foreign to each other, but with sovereign authority over their respective territories – was acknowledged. The policy statement of the Brandt government in October 1969 described the objective thus: 'Even if there exist two states in Germany, they cannot be foreign countries to each other; their mutual relations can only be of a special nature.'[19]

The Basic Treaty included a renunciation of force declaration, respect by the GDR for four power rights in Berlin, the relinquishment by the Federal Republic of the claim to represent all Germans, and respect by Bonn for East Berlin's autonomy. 'Permanent representative' missions were to be exchanged but not embassies as that would imply full legal recognition. As in the Moscow Treaty, East Berlin accepted a letter from Bonn enunciating the long-term goal of eventual German reunification in circumstances of free self-determination. Another exchange of letters noted that both states would seek membership of the United Nations. The Basic Treaty also included a variety of humanitarian elements, detailed in further exchanges of letters, regarding easing travel between the two states, reducing problems of family separation, and so on.

All through the negotiations Moscow had been putting firm pressure on East Berlin to reach agreement before the November 1972 elections in the Federal Republic, where a successful outcome for the SPD/FDP coalition was essential to the success of the overall Ostpolitik package. A further incentive for Moscow to encourage the successful outcome to Brandt's Ostpolitik was the fillip it would give to Brezhnev's plans for a European security conference – which would multilateralize the fundamental achievements of Ostpolitik, give the arrangements the regional stamp of approval, and provide a high profile platform for what Moscow assessed as the major Soviet foreign policy achievement in Europe since 1945. Brezhnev had invested considerable personal political capital in *détente*. The clutch of Ostpolitik treaties, SALT I (signed in May 1972), growing East–West economic relations and a successful European security conference would vindicate and strengthen his personal political position in the Soviet Union.

A vital feature of *détente* in Europe at this time for the Western allies as well as for the Federal Republic was the position of Berlin, and in particular the security of West Berlin. The whole Berlin issue acted as a brake on the pace of Brandt's Ostpolitik. Without signs of progress in the Berlin talks the Moscow and Warsaw treaties of 1970 would have come to nought, and the Western allies would have strongly discouraged Bonn in its new approach. President Nixon, while visiting West Berlin in 1969, had expressed support for a reduction of tensions and a regularization of four-power arrangements in the city. This was noted by the Soviets, and four power Berlin talks paralleled the Moscow–Bonn Treaty talks. Berlin was not part of the Moscow Treaty, as legally it is a four power responsibility, but the Soviet Union was well aware of the Federal Republic's insistence that agreements on Berlin must be part of the overall package. There was no legal linkage, but there was real political linkage. In September 1971 the new Quadripartite Agreement on Berlin was concluded, and signed by Moscow in June 1972 following ratification of the Moscow and Warsaw treaties by the Bundestag.

Over ten years after the construction of the notorious Berlin wall, agreement was reached on the status of the city, the rights of the occupying powers and of the Federal Republic and the GDR, transit rights to West Berlin from the Federal Republic, and increased levels of human contact between East and West Berlin, the Federal Republic and East Berlin and the GDR. The Western allies retained supreme authority in the Western sectors of the city. On the issue of transit rights, long the bone of contention and an instrument of coercion in Soviet hands in 1948–49 and 1958–61, the Soviet Union 'assumed the responsibility for preserving unimpeded Western access across the intervening East German territory, thus relinquishing the claim that West Berlin was really on the territory of its German satellite'.[20] In return, the Western allies agreed that West Berlin was not an integral, political part of the Federal Republic, though there was and is a close relationship – what Bonn would call 'ties' and Moscow, 'links'.[21] Bonn was supposed to refrain from holding political meetings there such as the Bundesrat, but on occasion has not complied with that part of the agreement. Of considerable humanitarian importance, however, ease of travel for West Berliners to East Berlin and the German Democratic Republic was considerably improved – an immense advance which Brandt was delighted to stress in his support for the Quadripartite Agreement. East Berlin was not all that happy with the agreement, as it obliged closer contact with the Federal Republic, but given Soviet and Polish enthusiasm, East Berlin was increasingly isolated in this respect. A trade agreement between the Federal Republic and the Soviet Union in April 1972 included West Berlin, thereby underlining Soviet eagerness to ease tensions and to include West Berlin in the overall *détente*, so long as a complete package deal was agreed.

The final element of the Ostpolitik package was the Bonn–Prague Treaty of December 1973. This came right at the end of the process of accommodation with the East primarily because, following the Bonn–Warsaw Treaty, the negotiations with the GDR took so long. The heart of the problem between the Federal Republic and Czechoslovakia was the Munich Agreement of 1938, which had never been officially rescinded. Also, even five years after the invasion, the Czechoslovakian government and the Czechoslovakian Communist Party were still experiencing close Soviet control. Under the Federal Republic–Czechoslovakian Treaty of December 1973, the Munich Agreement was finally declared null and void. This had practical legal consequences regarding the citizenship of Czechoslovakian Germans native to the previously disputed Sudeten territories which Hitler had annexed.[22]

By 1974 the formal treaty-making phase of Bonn's Ostpolitik was completed. The two Germanies were members of the United Nations, and the Federal Republic had opened formal diplomatic relations with all the members of the Warsaw Pact except the GDR, with which it has special diplomatic relations. In this era of *détente* the Federal Republic was contributing to an easing of tensions and accommodating to geopolitical realities, rather than attempting any radical rearrangements. Concomitant with the Federal Republic's accommodation and that of the Western allies in Berlin, multilateral processes, politically linked to the Ostpolitik, were also under way in Europe. The Soviet Union was keen to hold a grand European security conference, while the West supported a military conference on force levels in central Europe.

Before carrying on to an examination of these parallel developments, it is worth assessing the consequences of the Ostpolitik of the early 1970s, the primary political result of which was the practical recognition of the territorial and political status quo in central and East Europe prevalent since Potsdam. This included the division of Germany and the loss of a quarter of the 1938 German state. In reality the Ostpolitik treaties acknowledged the hegemony of the Soviet Union in East Europe and the permanent division of Germany for the foreseeable future. On the credit side, for the Federal Republic many of the political inhibitions felt by the new state were considerably diluted. Being a treaty partner, especially with the major ideological and military adversary of the Second World War, contributed to

German international rehabilitation. In the world of *realpolitik*, Brandt's Ostpolitik greatly increased Bonn's freedom of man-oeuvre and independence *vis-à-vis* the West as well as the East. By renouncing immediate demands for reunification with the GDR and the recovery of lost eastern territories, Bonn removed the leverage which its Western allies could exert over Bonn's political behaviour. As East–West *détente* progressed, the Western allies could no longer raise before Bonn the spectre of Western dealings with the East European states with which Bonn and its allies were in dispute:

> by resolving this 'special conflict' with the East, the Federal Republic has also lightened the burden of its dependence on the West. The refusal to sanctify the post-war status quo and to recognise East Germany could only be sustained with the unflagging help of West Germany's Western allies. Their solidarity exacted a steep price. For over two decades FRG foreign policy was marked by a degree of loyalty, deference, and even submission to the key Western powers rarely seen in the history of alliance politics.[23]

Such political release, coupled with economic strength, greatly enhanced the Federal Republic's political influence and status in Europe and in East–West relations in the mid 1970s. By 1975 Bonn was contributing 30 per cent of the EEC budget, recovering only 12 per cent in return. The Federal Republic's gross national product was greater than any of its EEC partners. Bonn emerged as the pay master of the EEC, an organization in which the Federal Republic played a leading role in the decade 1975–85. However, West German industry and commerce have not been solely preoccupied with business in the West in recent years. The Ostpolitik reopened German markets to the East from which West German trade had been excluded for most of the Cold War period. By 1978 trade between the two Germanies amounted to 8.8 billion Deutschmarks, excluding travel between the Federal Republic and the German Democratic Republic which, it is reckoned, netted the GDR a further 1 billion Deutschmarks. Between 1970 and 1976 West German foreign trade doubled: in East Europe it more than doubled. Trade with the Soviet Union quadrupled in this period, and with Poland and Hungary increased nearly as much. By 1979 exports to the Soviet Union were exceeding those to the United States. By the end of the 1970s, West German trade with the CMEA nearly exceeded that with the United States. The Federal Republic exports more finished products to the Soviet Union than any other Western country, and in return raw materials, most notably large supplies of natural gas and 40 per cent of its imports of enriched uranium, are secured.[24] By the 1980s the markets to the East have become a vital and valuable element of the West German economy, and it is reckoned that about 10 per cent of the West German workforce is employed in trade with these rediscovered markets.

The humanitarian features of Ostpolitik are generally acknowledged to constitute a major tangible success. Within six months of the signing of the Warsaw Treaty in December 1970, over 50,000 ethnic Germans were repatriated to the Federal Republic from Poland. Between 1972 and 1979 approximately 200,000 ethnic Germans were allowed to leave the Soviet Union and East Europe. In the same period about 50,000 East Germans were allowed to join their families in the West.[25] Willy Brandt details some of the human benefits thus:

> The number of visitors from Federal territory to the GDR doubled in the course of five years to more than three million. In 1975, over 400,000 people took advantage of the newly established 'minor frontier traffic' facilities between the Federal Republic and the GDR. Visits from the GDR by 'persons of pensionable age' rose from 1 to 1.3 million. A substantial number of GDR citizens were granted travel permits for 'pressing family reasons'. The number of telephone lines between the two German states rose from 34 to over 700. Gift parcel traffic services became easier.[26]

Politically, economically and socially, Ostpolitik has been of benefit to the Federal Republic. There is also a strong argument that the Warsaw Pact has gained considerably from it. To ask which side has gained the most may be a fascinating exercise, but not very productive. Both wished to reduce tensions in central Europe in pursuance of different objectives. For instance, the Soviet Union wanted West German recognition of the status quo in central and East Europe prior to and as an impetus towards a

European security conference; it also wished to advance its economic links with the Federal Republic. In these regards the Soviet Union waged a successful policy. This does not mean that the Federal Republic or the West were losers, because Ostpolitik was not a zero-sum game. The Federal Republic did not fall out of step with the process of East–West *détente*. Ostpolitik brought considerable economic advantage to the West German economy and improved the social conditions of many Germans throughout Europe. Certainly, any hope of reunification in the short term was abandoned, but such a prospect was not at all likely anyway. One of the things Brandt's Ostpolitik did do was to establish a formal political relationship between the two Germanies far in advance of the bitterness of the previous twenty years.

However, such are the economic, social and political links of the Federal Republic with the East, and such is its confidence *vis-à-vis* its allies on the international stage, that some commentators are prone to suggest that the 'Finlandization' of the Federal Republic was a Soviet objective. It is often argued that such are the FRG's interests in the East that it is loathe to jeopardize them by criticizing Soviet behaviour as vehemently as it ought or by taking concrete action when required, and that a wedge has been driven between the Federal Republic and the rest of the Alliance, especially the United States. West German insistence on continuing with the Siberian gas pipeline in the wake of the invasion of Afghanistan, its reluctance to impose economic sanctions on Poland following the banning of Solidarity and the declaration of martial law in 1981, and Schmidt's pressure on the Reagan administration to undertake arms control discussions with the Soviet Union, are cited as demonstrations of West German reluctance to stand firm with the West and of the 'hostage' effect of its eastern interests on its foreign policy. Spectres of the Rapallo Treaty of 1922 and the Molotov-Ribbentrop Pact of 1939, when Germany surprised and shocked the world by turning to the Soviet Union for security arrangements and trade relations, have been raised by some alarmists.[27] But, in sharp contrast to today, in those two historic cases Germany had been abandoned by or was in political conflict with the West. There was nowhere else to turn. Today, the Federal Republic is firmly integrated into the Western community of states. Even if Moscow was to completely change its policies of the past thirty years and offer the FRG reunification in return for a clear move towards the East, an appalling political, economic and social price would be paid. For the foreseeable future it is inconceivable that the Federal Republic would voluntarily leave NATO or the EEC.

The Ostpolitik treaties recognized geopolitical reality in Europe. For the leading, front-line member of NATO not to have done so would have weakened rather than sustained the West. The Federal Republic emerged from the process the stronger, and with power and influence much more commensurate with its strategic position and economic achievements. Undoubtedly, in European *détente* the Federal Republic has more at stake than any other Alliance member, and Bonn's perspective is bound, on occasions, to be different from that prevalent in Washington. Given that Bonn is placed at the heart of the arena of conflict, competition and cooperation, rather than thousands of miles across the Atlantic Ocean, differences of emphasis and inter- pretation on complex matters of East–West relations between Bonn and Washington should hardly be surprising. But when toughness is required, Bonn stands firm. The support of Helmut Schmidt and subsequent West German governments and electo- rates for the NATO decision of 1979 to deploy modernized INF in West Europe is a vivid illustration of the Federal Republic's commitment to Western values and security.

Conference on Security and Cooperation in Europe (CSCE)

A major public element of the geopolitical accommodation between East and West in Europe has been the Conference on Security and Cooperation in Europe which began with prepara- tory talks in Helsinki in November 1972. Following a lengthy second phase at Geneva between September 1973 and July 1975, where most of the hard discussion and bargaining took place, it produced, in a third stage, the famous Final Act in Helsinki on 31 July and 1 August 1975. At Helsinki thirty-five countries – all of Europe (except Albania) and the United States and Canada – signed the Final Act, which, because it did not have the status of international law, was called an act and not a treaty. Neverthe-less, the Final Act did create considerable expectations that the relaxation of tensions experienced in Europe and between the superpowers in the years 1970–75 had laid the foundations for a new era of cooperation and coexistence between the rival blocs. In reality, Helsinki 1975 was a plateau from which few new peaks of East–West cooperation and understanding were scaled. Indeed, many conservative elements would argue that there was then a descent in *détente*. Such perceptions stem, in part, from disappointments over the dividends yielded in the human rights field by the Helsinki Act. Helsinki 1975 was a symbolic conference, but in many people's minds it created expectations which an ideologically hide-bound Eastern bloc could not deliver.

In reality the effect and the purpose of the CSCE in Soviet minds was to underpin the geopolitical status quo in Europe not to undermine it. The Ostpolitik agreements of 1970–73 appeared to remove a need for a general European security conference. Relations between the West and East Europe regarding issues such as the recognition of the German Democratic Republic, the regularization of West Berlin's status, and the status of postwar frontiers seemed to have been resolved before 1975.[28] But the Soviet Union pressed for a multilateral conference. A continental affirmation of the boundaries created by the Red Army's military victories in 1945, and, *ipso facto*, a recognition of Soviet hegemony in East Europe, had long been a major Soviet foreign policy objective.

Soviet proposals for a European security conference had begun between Stalin's death and the Geneva summit of 1955. In the days of the Cold War, United States nuclear superiority and implacable West German opposition to any agreement even hinting at recognition of the German Democratic Republic's and Poland's post-1945 boundaries, meant that there was little prospect of a conference to ratify the Soviet Union's European policies. Only in the late 1960s, with the onset of superpower *détente* and the realization in the West that the Soviet Union's East European client system was not about to disintegrate under Western pressure or – as the intervention in Czechoslovakia in 1968 clearly demonstrated – be allowed to liberalize itself politically, did the West begin to respond positively to Soviet overtures.

In West Europe some states saw the conference as a mechanism to influence the pace and direction of *détente*, and to avoid leaving the Federal Republic and United States alone together in the driving seat. Also, there were urgings by some East European states that a European security conference might impose some control on the scope of the Brezhnev Doctrine, used by the Soviets to legitimize their actions in Czechoslovakia.[29] In addition to discussing political facets of European security, which was the major objective of the Soviet Union, the Western powers were determined to initiate discussion on arms control in Europe. By 1972 it was agreed that two conferences would begin in 1973: one, a conference on European security and cooperation, which would include the United States and Canada as participants and put human rights on the agenda, and the other, a conference between NATO and the Warsaw Pact on force reductions in central Europe. The CSCE began in Helsinki in November 1972, and in January 1973 the arms talks known in the West as the Mutual and Balanced Force Reduction (MBFR) talks began in Vienna.

For the Soviet Union the major achievement of the CSCE was the Western reaffirmation of the territorial status quo in Europe. From the mid-1950s a major Soviet foreign policy objective had been not to dismantle the blocs in Europe, but to get the West to confirm the bloc structure. 'Basket I' of the Final Act, on security relations between states, did just that – 'the participating states regard as inviolable each other's frontiers, as well as the frontiers of all states in Europe.'[30] This 'basket' also includes renunciation of the use of force to settle disputes between states. At Helsinki the West did not give anything away which had not already been lost or ceded many years before, and the international behaviour proscribed by the Final Act was contrary to international law anyway: 'It is hard to see a sell-out in the Helsinki agreements (mostly attacked by those who have not read them). The West did not "recognise" the Soviet sphere of influence, it merely restated what was already in the United Nations Charter and countless other documents – that force would not be used to change borders.'[31] Indeed, Soviet enthusiasm for a European conference provided the West with some useful leverage. The Federal Republic refused to support the CSCE until relations with the German Democratic Republic were settled. This increased the pressure from Moscow on East Berlin to accommodate with Bonn.[32] Furthermore, at the insistence of the West Europeans two non-European states became an integral part of the CSCE process, and the signatures of Gerald Ford and Pierre Trudeau along with Leonid Brezhnev on the Final Act acknowledged the legitimate interests of the United States and Canada in European security. This helped cement rather than fragment North American–West European relations.

'Basket II' of the Final Act, covering economic, scientific and cultural cooperation, was again a recognition of what was already happening. There had been a surge of trade across the Iron Curtain in the 1970s, and scientific and cultural exchange was, in carefully selected areas, increasing. Helsinki reaffirmed that this was desirable.

A major impact of the Final Act has been the controversy created by the 'Basket III' clauses on human rights in Europe, and the human rights element in the introductory declaration to the Final Act.[33] The net effect of Soviet attitudes to human rights in East Europe since 1975, Soviet disregard for the human rights stipulations of the Final Act and, generally, the cautious though occasionally robust Western response, all demonstrate the commitment of both blocs to a perpetuation of the rigid bloc system in Europe. In the eyes of many Western supporters of *détente*, the outstanding achievement of the Final Act was the human rights component. This was going to oblige the Warsaw Pact states to open up their societies to internal reform, and facilitate freer contact with the West. For instance, part of Clause VII of the Final Act states:

> The participating States will respect human rights and fundamental freedoms, including the freedom of thought, conscience, religion or belief, for all without distinction as to race, sex, language or religion.
>
> They will promote and encourage the effective exercise of civil, political, economic, social, cultural and other rights and freedoms all of which derive from the inherent dignity

of the human person and are essential for his free and full development.[34]

The human rights clauses of the Final Act, for which the West traded recognition of the territorial status quo, are what marked out the CSCE for world-wide attention, and the world, especially the peoples of the West, waited to see what would happen. The man in the street and some crusading politicians anticipated the liberalization of East Europe. But this is not what the Soviets intended. And none of those deeply involved in the conference expected much progress either. Yet, to a considerable extent, the value of the CSCE has come to be measured by Communist compliance with the Final Act's human rights stipulations:

> This theme – the test of implementation – was the single most prominent one at the Helsinki summit and suggested that the CSCE, originally an Eastern bloc proposal, had been significantly turned around. In the end, it imposed a largely Western set of values as a measuring stick for the advancement of the Helsinki spirit. None of the participants, however, believed implementation would be immediate or far reaching.[35]

Many of the human rights ideals contained in the Final Act are also integral to many constitutions in East Europe, not least that of the Soviet Union. But little has been achieved in the advancement of such ideals. The Warsaw Pact signatories of the Final Act were obliged to publish it in their newspapers – which did create expectation among some sectors of the populations, especially the intelligentsia. Unofficial groups such as Charter 77 in Czechoslovakia, the Helsinki watch committees in the Soviet Union and the Workers' Defence Committee in Poland were established to capitalize on 'Basket III' and attempt to influence liberalization in their societies. But few of the regimes have tolerated high-profile activity by such groups, and periodically they have been harassed, members have been arrested and imprisoned and, in the case of the Soviet Helsinki watch committees, finally coerced out of existence. 'Basket III' has been an unexpected nuisance within Eastern societies, but no more than a nuisance. The authority of the Communist Party in all Warsaw Pact countries, except Poland, remains firm and unchallenged. Indeed, more than ten years after the Final Act there is dispute over the net effect on European security of its human rights provisions. It could be argued that occasional surges of public concern in the West, especially in the United States, over individual human rights in the East provoked the regimes into clamping down on whatever limited room for manoeuvre the dissidents may have:

> As radical as many of these intellectuals may be in the eyes of Communist party functionaries, they are careful to safeguard their own manoeuvrability. They guard jealously their ability to write, publish, or teach. Many of these intellectuals believe that confrontation over Helsinki or President Carter's human rights doctrine has become counter-productive. They are embarrassed by the early Carter administration policy of singling out their situation while ignoring violations by America's allies or friends. They feel that the progress and the tempo of demands for expanded human rights is something they must control themselves.[36]

There is a view that too much pressure on the Eastern bloc over human rights is counterproductive – that a souring of East–West relations over the human rights situation and 'a return to Cold War would doom any chances for it'[37] – while at least *détente* creates some prospect of liberalization. But the prospect of liberalization has so excited many actors in the Western body politic that failure by the Soviet bloc to abide by the human rights elements of the Final Act has created distrust about the whole *détente* process and about Soviet intentions.[38] In addition, attempts to use whatever leverage might be available to oblige the East to fulfil their promises have hindered the implementation of *détente*. Concepts of linkage – sometimes against the wishes of the United States' government, sometimes not – have seriously disturbed East–West relations and created division in the West. As noted earlier, the year following the Final Act President Ford was forced to drop the word '*détente*' from his election campaign for the presidency, and Reagan supporters were able to include anti-*détente* planks in the party platform. On the other hand, American liberals were strongly critical of Kissinger for not putting enough pressure on the Soviet Union over its violations of human rights.[39]

Another feature of the division created by the human rights issue has been the difference of perspective in West Europe from that in the United States. The West European approach to the subject is much more low-key and much more utilitarian – improvement in the quality of life for the largest possible numbers rather than concentration on the plight of individual intellectuals. There has been a tendency in the United States, under the Carter and Reagan administrations, to focus on individual political human rights problems and to create a furore over the plights of certain dissidents, such as Anatoly Shcharansky, Yuri Orlov or Andrei Sakharov. West Europeans would argue that this results in a harder social and cultural climate for the majority of the population, and that dissident intellectuals are repressed as a result of too much public pressure from Washington. The CSCE Review Conference held at Belgrade in 1977–78, and the Madrid Review Conference of 1980–83, illustrate this Atlantic difference of opinion in contrasting ways. At Belgrade the Carter administration deliberately down-played the human rights violations of the Soviet bloc in deference to the wishes of the West Europeans. It was clear that not everyone in the US delegation was happy at this tactic, but the White House and the State Department were determined to go along with the West European allies, who were fearful of the brittle nature of *détente* in Europe.[40] The question of compliance with the Final Act was raised publicly in only the most general way, while individual cases were dealt with in private sessions. The final document of the Belgrade Review Conference glossed over human rights failures in the Soviet bloc, stating only that different views were expressed and that the participating states could not reach a consensus. The major accomplishment of the Belgrade conference was to keep *détente* on the rails, and to agree a date and place for the next CSCE review conference – Madrid in 1980.

At Madrid the United States was determined to be much more robust. The overall climate of East–West relations had deteriorated considerably in the years since Belgrade, primarily because of the Soviet invasion of Afghanistan in 1979, the build-up of Soviet military power, the abandonment of the formal ratification process for the SALT II Treaty in the United States (although both superpowers have since behaved as though it had been ratified) and the continued human rights violations in the Soviet bloc. While the Madrid conference was under way, Solidarity rose to prominence, only to be repressed by the military coup of December 1981. In November 1980, the month the conference began, Ronald Reagan defeated President Carter in the presidential elections.

The United States was most frank in its criticism of the behaviour of the Soviet Union, often to the consternation of some of its West European allies, who did not always concur with Washington's interpretation of events. For instance, the Schmidt administration in Bonn did not agree with the Reagan administration's assessment of the role of the Soviet Union in the military coup in Poland. And such was the acrimony between the superpowers themselves at Madrid that the Review Conference dragged on for three years. In an effort to distract attention from Afghanistan and human rights issues, the Soviet Union chose to concentrate on military–security issues in Europe, and Poland suggested a European disarmament conference – a proposal short on specific objectives and procedures. A previous French proposal, with its roots in an idea of Giscard d'Estaing's in 1978, was much more detailed.[41] The West Europeans, in return for agreeing to devote some of their attention to the plight of Solidarity, managed to persuade the United States to go along with the discussions on European disarmament proposals.[42]

The Madrid Review Conference came to an end in September 1983. It ended as it had been conducted all along, amidst much acrimony – this time over the shooting down by a Soviet war plane of a South Korean civilian airliner, off-course over part of the Soviet Pacific coast. However, Madrid did produce advances on Helsinki and was much more productive than Belgrade, which lasted only six months. Amongst other things, the Madrid concluding document supported the rights of workers to establish trade unions, and called on states to sustain dialogue with religious organizations in their countries. These clauses were the clear result of United States pressure over the situation in

Poland; but, as with the Final Act, there is little real prospect of the Western interpretation of these objectives being followed. Another important feature of Madrid was the decision to go ahead with a conference on confidence-building measures in the military field which, given the limited agreement on similar measures at Helsinki in 1975, and their occasional implementation by the Warsaw Pact, may hold out a prospect of something concrete being achieved. Again, this is a process aimed at enhancing the security of the rival blocs and reinforcing the rigidity of the bloc structure, not at dismantling it.

In January 1984 the Conference on Disarmament in Europe (CDE) began in Stockholm (full title – the Conference on Confidence and Security-Building Measures and Disarmament in Europe). To focus solely on the disarmament feature of the title is misleading, as the business of the conference comprises primarily confidence-building measures rather than efforts at real disarmament. CDE is very much part of the Helsinki process, and its achievements will be evaluated at the next CSCE review conference in Vienna in 1986. Its roots go back not just to the Madrid conference, which called for confidence- and security-building measures (CSBMs) that should be 'of military significance and politically binding and ... provided with adequate forms of verification',[43] but right back to the Helsinki Final Act. CSBMs are meant to enhance security and boost confidence by reducing fears of sudden attack and suspicions about the military behaviour of the other side, though not necessarily by reducing the actual forces deployed. The Helsinki Final Act sowed the seeds of this approach when it required all thirty-five member states to give twenty-one days' advance notice of major military manoeuvres involving more than 25,000 troops, and suggested regular exchanges of military observers. James Goodby, ambassador and head of the United States' delegation to the CDE in Stockholm, described the purpose of the new talks thus:

> The Stockholm Conference is different from 'classical' arms control negotiations in that it addresses not the capabilities for war, the number of weapons and troops, but rather the most likely causes of war: flawed judgements or miscalcula-

tions stemming from fears of sudden attack and uncertainty about the military intentions of an adversary. It is highly unlikely that any war at all will commence in Europe. But if war should ever come, it probably would not be in the form of a 'bolt-from-the-blue' attack by one side against another. The most probable cause of the outbreak of war would be some small incident, perhaps connected with a military manoeuvre, which would not be clearly understood, leading to confrontation and armed conflict. This nightmare is an improbable scenario but the stakes are so high that some reassurance against such a contingency would be in everyone's interest. If it is successful, the Stockholm Conference will negotiate and put into place certain procedures which could stop a fatal progression towards catastrophe.

Procedures which would make military activities in Europe more predictable would reassure governments that those activities were normal, routine and non-threatening. Procedures for questioning and verifying the essential character of specific military activities would provide more certain knowledge of the intentions of the parties to this agreement. Such reassurance would lead to increased confidence and security among all participating states.[44]

Between 1975 and 1984 there were about one hundred notifications of military activities in Europe involving over two million troops. But not all manoeuvres have been notified. The largest manoeuvre in the past ten years – unnotified – has been the Soviet Union's Zapad 81, in the Soviet Union near the Polish border, at a very tense period in Polish–Soviet relations. Observers have been invited to approximately fifty exercises. The West has extended more than thirty invitations, and the United States alone has issued ten. The Warsaw Pact has notified more than twenty manoeuvres, but issued invitations to attend less than half. United States observers have been invited to only two Warsaw Pact manoeuvres, and none at all since 1979.[45] An interesting feature of the CDE – unlike the Final Act, whose zone of application extended only 250 kilometres into the

Soviet Union – is that the whole of Europe from the Atlantic to the Urals is to be included in the zone of application. This, however, has created some contention: a major controversial issue is the geographical zone to which CSBMs will apply. In return for extending the Helsinki zone of application all the way to the Urals, the Warsaw Pact wants to include European and North Atlantic waters, in an effort to counter NATO maritime strength.[46] There are considerable practical attractions to considering the whole of Europe as the zone of application at the CDE. As the MBFR negotiations at Vienna have demonstrated for over ten years, an artificial limitation to a few countries or parts of countries in Europe is politically and militarily counterproductive. It discriminates politically against some countries and militarily it makes confidence in the outcome of negotiations difficult to sustain because of the high mobility of modern armies. Intrusions by military reinforcements into any prospective, limited CSBM zone of application would be very easy in modern Europe.

The NATO aim is to create 'transparency' in both blocs: the objectives of military activities would be clear to either side through obligatory exchanges of information. For instance, under NATO proposals, which would be mandatory, there would be an annual exchange of information giving details of the structure of ground and air forces in all of Europe, including unit designation, normal headquarters locations and composition of forces. Also, the NATO proposal calls for forty five days' advance notification of activities involving in-the-field training of units at division level or above, and notification of certain mobilization and amphibious exercises. Furthermore, NATO has called for means of urgent East–West communications to be improved.[47] The Warsaw Pact is inclined to view such proposals as a spying exercise. 'Legalized espionage' is a Soviet term often used. The Soviet Union prefers to seek multilateral pledges such as no first use of nuclear weapons, and declarations of nuclear-free zones. NATO sees such pledges as meaningless and unenforceable.

It is clear that the objectives of both major blocs at the CDE is to sustain security and stability in Europe. It is not to take risks in challenging the geopolitical status quo, but to make that status quo less prone to accidental conflict arising from misinterpretation of adversary intentions. Each major bloc has its own perspective of what CDE outcome best suits its longer-term political goals. But it is not the policy of either bloc to use the CDE to destabilize the bloc system in Europe. Their different perspectives have been accommodated by the establishment of two working groups, one dealing largely with the East's proposals and the other with the West's. The plan is that some day both sets of proposals will be considered together.

M(B)FR

The moribund Mutual Force Reduction (MFR) talks in Vienna, in progress since October 1973, illustrate the geopolitical focus of the blocs. In the West the talks are often known as the Mutual and Balanced Force Reduction (MBFR) talks, but in 1973 the West agreed to drop the concept of 'balanced' reductions in return for the inclusion of 'associated measures'. Now, in Europe, they are officially called talks on the 'mutual reduction of forces and armaments and associated measures'. What the West had in mind was the discussion of CSBMs such as those in the CSCE Final Act and those which form the focus of discussion in Stockholm at the moment. But over the past twelve years or more of the talks, the focus has been exclusively on numbers of troops and, on occasions, tanks. Even given the political will, this has not been conducive to reaching a worthwhile agreement.

Since 1973 there have been a number of initiatives from both blocs to limit the numbers of forces in the MFR zone of application.[48] In the West this zone is known as the NATO guideline area (NGA), and includes the Federal Republic, the German Democratic Republic, Poland, Czechoslovakia and the Benelux countries. The progress of these talks in the 1970s demonstrates the problems encountered and the futility of the numbers approach.

In October 1973 NATO made an initial proposal to establish approximate parity between the two sides in the form of a common manpower ceiling for overall ground forces in the NGA. The first phase was to be the withdrawal, outside the NGA, of

29,000 US troops, and of 68,000 Soviet troops (the equivalent of a Soviet tank army) from East Germany. This would represent, according to NATO's figures, a 15 per cent reduction in both the US and Soviet forces in the NGA. A second phase was to be composed of negotiations aimed at reductions to a common ceiling of 700,000 troops, for both alliances, in the NGA. The perceived Warsaw Pact superiority on the ground was the focus of NATO's proposals – and hence its suggestion for asymmetrical cuts. The fact that Soviet forces would be withdrawn to the western Soviet Union, only a few hundred miles from the heart of the NGA, while US forces would return to North America, and that NATO had already agreed to the exclusion of Hungary from the NGA, where 55,000 Soviet troops are stationed, did not make the NATO offer attractive, and the Warsaw Pact rejected it. Its argument was that forces in the NGA are roughly equal, that cuts should be on an equal percentage basis and not restricted to ground and conventional forces only, that indigenous European forces be included, and that national sub-ceilings should be established. In all probability the Bundeswehr was the target of the last proposal. Hence in 1973 the Warsaw Pact proposals were as follows:

Phase I　　　a reduction by both alliances of 20,000 troops
Phase II　　　a further 5 per cent reduction
Phase III　　a further 10 per cent reduction

From NATO's perspective the implementation of such a proposal would merely have perpetuated the imbalance of forces, and possibly reduced NATO forces to below a minimum secure, operable level.

Two years of virtual deadlock followed the stalemate of October 1973; then in 1975 the West submitted an altered proposal which broadened the scope of the negotiations. NATO proposed the withdrawal of 1,000 tactical nuclear warheads, 54 nuclear capable F-4 aircraft, 36 Pershing SS missiles and 29,000 US troops. The ceiling envisaged was 900,000 men (sub-ceilings of 700,000 for ground forces and 200,000 for air forces) in the NGA. No reciprocal nuclear reduction was requested from the Soviet forces in the NGA, but NATO still proposed the removal of a Soviet tank army from the German Democratic Republic. This Western proposal was rejected because it was seen to be inadequate on forward-based systems; the issue of equal percentage as opposed to asymmetrical reductions was not resolved and the Soviets still pressed, *inter alia*, for national sub-ceilings. To many commentators in the West such Soviet tactics appeared to reveal that Moscow was treating MFR as a political exercise, outside the spirit of *détente*, rather than as a meaningful arms control negotiation.

However, in June 1976, six months after NATO's December 1975 proposal, some progress was made in that the Warsaw Pact submitted data on force levels (something it had previously declined to do), but the figures were at variance with NATO estimates of Warsaw Pact strength in the NGA:

	NATO estimate	*WP estimate*
WP ground forces	925,000	805,000
WP tactical air forces	204,000	160,000

In March 1978 the Warsaw Pact submitted additional detailed data, but large discrepancies remained. The following month NATO submitted a new proposal which now accepted the principle of equal percentage cuts, but after approximate parity had been reached. The new proposal required the removal of any 1,700 tanks and 68,000 troops from any five Soviet divisions in the NGA, rather than specifically from East Germany. In return, two thirds of the 29,000 US troops could be taken from selected units, plus 1,000 nuclear warheads. One criticism of this proposal, voiced in the West, was that in any agreement Moscow could remove manpower from well behind the inner-German border but still in the NGA, and include only its oldest tanks. The elite units in the German Democratic Republic, the immediate threat to NATO's central front, would be left untouched. In the April President Carter decided not to proceed with the production of the enhanced radiation weapon (neutron bomb), viewed essentially as a mass tank-killing weapon, and many criticized this as the needless sacrifice of a potential MFR bargaining chip, particularly as the East made no reciprocal move.

In the summer of 1978 the Warsaw Pact indicated that they now accepted the principle of parity in manpower and NATO's target ceilings as enunciated in December 1975. Importantly, the

East also claimed to accept the collectivity principle. In a first phase the Eastern bloc proposed a reduction of only 1,000 tanks and 30,000 men and as, according to their figures, approximate parity already existed, Warsaw Pact forces would not need to be cut more than NATO ground forces to bring down both alliances to a 700,000 ground forces level. NATO rejected the offer.

The 1980s have not been any more productive. The MFR talks are still in progress in Vienna. The data question remains to be resolved: the West still insists that the Warsaw Pact is understating its troops in the NGA by 150,000 men. The data obstacle has been, and remains, the outstanding impediment to any meaningful progress in Vienna. In March 1978 East and West had presented disaggregated data which revealed that the discrepancy was rooted in Soviet and Polish forces;[49] in January 1980 the data was updated, but the discrepancy remained. Different counting rules may account for the discrepancy. The West counts all personnel wearing army uniform as ground forces, whereas the East has a functional counting rule: that is, all personnel performing a ground forces function are counted. There may be others in uniform, but if they do not perform a ground forces function they are not counted.[50] Efforts by both sides to achieve a first phase withdrawal of ground forces have not managed to overcome the data discrepancy issue. A Western attempt to side-step this problem is currently under discussion: the West has agreed that, temporarily, the data dispute be set aside, but that a limited withdrawal of forces be linked to a stringent and credible verification procedure.[51] What sort of verification procedures will be acceptable to the Warsaw Pact remains to be seen. It is not improbable that the MFR talks, unless they yield some concrete results in the near future, could be incorporated into the CDE at Stockholm. Increased discussion of verification procedures, and attempts by the West to include CSBMs (which have always been on the MFR agenda but received secondary consideration) in the Vienna talks, would make the CDE the natural forum for such negotiations.

In reality the primary purpose of MFR for both blocs has been to reinforce political objectives rather than to reduce the military forces of the alliances. In 1971 there was considerable pressure in Washington, led by Senator Mike Mansfield, for the unilateral reduction of United States forces in Europe, and a Congressional action to that effect was very nearly successful. The Nixon administration used the prospect of force reductions talks to insist that any reductions should take place within an East–West framework:

> The pressures for unilateral withdrawal of US forces from the FRG, led by Senator Mike Mansfield, escalated, threatening a major disengagement of US forces from Europe. MBFR provided the Nixon Administration with an argument for delay – why proceed with unilateral withdrawals of US forces from Germany when those forces could be used as bargaining chips in negotiations designed to reduce the level of Soviet forces in Eastern Europe? Although this argument was designed primarily for domestic consumption, it was also used effectively to influence the Allies to maintain their force levels in the face of pressures from their publics to cut defence budgets.[52]

It was not any real enthusiasm for *détente* that drove the US administration towards MFR talks but, as one analyst noted in 1972, 'the conviction that MBFR provides a useful formula to stem domestic pressure for unilateral reductions and, if some concessions must be made to these pressures, to get some Soviet reduction in return'.[53] The West European allies saw joint negotiations with the United States on troop levels in central Europe as reinforcing the American entanglement in West European security and, in the light of the Nixon Doctrine and Washington's efforts to relinquish commitments in south-east Asia, as reconfirming its commitment to NATO Europe. All the NATO allies hoped there would be some limitations imposed on Soviet conventional forces in the NGA, if for no other reason than to relieve the American pressure on the West Europeans to improve their conventional forces. The Federal Republic had a keen interest in the military implications of MFR, and saw the negotiations as a logical complement to Ostpolitik, bolstering the political *modus vivendi* achieved by Bonn's diplomatic openings to the East.

The Eastern bloc also had political objectives in launching the MFR talks. Moscow was fearful in the early 1970s that unilateral

United States troop withdrawals would rekindle enthusiasm for West European unity and, alarmingly, perhaps lead to a compensatory strengthening of the Bundeswehr, a subject of perpetual concern to Moscow since German rearmament. There are obvious historical reasons for such anxiety. Throughout the long process of the talks in Vienna there have been a number of attempts by the Warsaw Pact to impose sub-ceiling limits, within total NATO numbers, on Bundeswehr troop levels. This has always been resisted by NATO. A further attraction of MFR for Moscow is that troops released from East Europe could be re-deployed to the Far East on the Sino-Soviet border. Also, MFR provides a possible route into intra-NATO affairs. MFR is the only set of arms control talks directly between the alliances as institutions. Though it has not come to pass, there were Western fears in the early years that enticing offers from the Warsaw Pact could produce intra-NATO disagreement over how best to respond. However, the MFR talks in Vienna have been conducted in an environment of NATO solidarity. In the SALT I agreement of May 1972 Moscow had wished to include in the negotiations tactical nuclear weapons and NATO forward based (nuclear) systems (FBS) such as nuclear-capable aircraft, but the United States had insisted on restricting the agreement to intercontinental strategic nuclear systems. MFR was a forum where those original nuclear systems could be discussed. What is clear from the twelve years of MFR negotiations is that neither alliance ever envisaged the talks leading to major disarmament in central Europe, the eventual dismantling of the alliance bloc structure, or the redrawing of the political map of Europe. The real objective was to increase the security of the alliances and enhance the stability of the bloc structure in Europe, perhaps at lower force levels in the central region.

This chapter has examined the policies implemented and the mechanisms used by individual countries in Europe, and by the alliances, in coming to terms with the political and military realities of postwar Europe. Such geopolitical accommodation in Europe may have unattractive sociopolitical consequences – for example, the plight of Poland in the 1980s – but it appears to date to have been beneficial to European peace and security. Spheres of influence are clearly defined and guarded, and 'grey areas' are absent. East Europe, the scene of much historic German–Russian/Soviet rivalry, where both of the twentieth century's world wars have broken out, has been controlled and policed for the past forty years. The reunification of Germany, and the emergence of a Europe of nation-states from the Atlantic to the Urals, would engender great instability in East Europe. Historically, this region has been drawn economically towards Germany, but has been seen to be of vital strategic importance by Russia. Competition between these two regional great powers would be inevitable. For the remainder of this century such a scenario is most unlikely. While the Soviet hegemony exercised in East Europe has many unattractive features, it does at least ensure the absence of war arising out of German–Russian competition and conflict in this region. In Europe, at least, we ought to be grateful for the relative stability and security produced, in part, by a persistent attention to the requirements of the arms balance and mutual deterrence, and by the prudent and cautious behaviour of the states operating in the nuclear environment.

5

Prospects

In international politics accurate prediction is notoriously difficult. For instance, in the early 1950s who could have predicted the Sino-Soviet split ten years later, or in 1964 when the United States Congress passed the Gulf of Tonkin Resolution that within ten years the world's strongest military power would be abandoning its ally in south-east Asia after beating a hasty and humiliating military withdrawal, or that within three years the world would witness four general-secretaries of the CPSU? Nonetheless, given what is at stake in Europe, this final chapter will attempt to assess the prospects for the prevailing European security arrangements over the next ten to fifteen years, up to the end of the twentieth century. Such are the vagaries of the personal health and political fortune of politicians that no attempt will be made to assess developments in the field of political leadership. The challenges posed to the system will be identified and examined and, we hope, informed and balanced estimates made of the likely outcomes.

For over forty years there has been no inter-state war in Europe: a stable political and military balance between the rival European blocs has evolved. Prosperity has increased in both the East and the West, and particularly in the West. Political freedoms in the West have been safeguarded from external challenge, and there have been some net gains for democracy. The emergence of both Portugal and Spain from decades of Fascism, and the establishment and survival of democratic institutions in those countries, demonstrates the inherent attractions of liberal democracy and democratic capitalism on the European continent. Turkey, sitting astride the European–Asian divide, has encountered recurring difficulties in adapting its institutions to Western democracy, but, throughout its travails, no popular enthusiasm for Soviet-style Communism has been evinced. In the East some economic experimentation has occurred in Hungary and some idiosyncratic foreign policy has been practised by Rumania – a state of minor geostrategic importance to the Warsaw Pact, but with a very orthodox Communist domestic political system. In East Europe the rule that all political power remains in the hands of the Communist Party has been sacrosanct. To date, the coercive forces of the state apparatus throughout East Europe have sustained the pre-eminence of the Communist Party in the states which constitute the Warsaw Pact and has assured continued Soviet hegemony. The nuclear environment that envelopes East–West relations in Europe induces prudence and caution in bloc competition, and is the major reason for dialogue. But in the remaining few years of the twentieth century, may we expect the system to continue as in the previous four decades? What are the challenges posed to current European security arrangements?

At strategic nuclear level some pessimistic interpretations, particularly in the Pentagon, suggest that the Soviet superiority in land-based ICBMs provides a 'window of opportunity' for the Soviet Union, or a 'window of vulnerability' if viewed from the NATO perspective. Land-based ICBMs are the most accurate strategic nuclear weapons. Hypothetically, a first strike could knock out the US land-based ICBM force. This would leave the US with only its seaborne deterrent and bomber forces with which to respond. Until recently these have been the less accurate weapons systems, whose primary purpose has been to retaliate against Soviet cities. To do so, it could be argued, would then bring down on the United States the remainder of the Soviet strategic deterrent, land- and sea-based. No president would wish this to happen, so he would choose not to respond and to accept the major redistribution of the balance of world power which would follow the Soviet first strike. Of concern to the West Europeans in this improbable scenario is that the US strategic arsenal has traditionally extended deterrence to West Europe. A severely weakened US would be unable to do this, and West Europe would fall under Soviet sway. A major plank in the platform supporting SDI is an attempt to close this 'window of vulnerability'. However, this is indeed a highly improbable scenario. It is difficult to imagine a circumstance where a stable, rational Soviet leadership could take such horrendous risks. A Soviet first strike against US ICBM silos would result in at least 30 million American casualties. Relative to the total American population this could be termed 'limited', but it is hardly certain that the US government would not respond with whatever strategic nuclear weapons it had at its disposal. Anyway, if the Soviet leadership were unstable and irrational, then even superior US forces would not fulfil a deterrent function.

Concern over an inability to respond with only counter-force systems will soon diminish, as more Trident SSBNs and long-range cruise missiles are deployed. Such is the accuracy of these new systems that they may be deployed in counter-force roles if required. West European anxieties are being allayed by the deployment in Europe of US INF – systems which, from the Russo-strategic perspective, are strategic. The Soviet homeland is as vulnerable to US INF in Europe as it is to the US strategic arsenal outside Europe, if not more so. The same cannot be said of the American homeland, which is not vulnerable to Soviet INF. Also, the modernizing of the British and French independent strategic nuclear deterrents provide an indigenous, second 'West European' force of which the Soviets would have to take account in such a grave risk-taking calculation as to consider a first strike against US land-based counter-force strategic nuclear systems. There is a crude strategic nuclear parity between the United States and the Soviet Union in intercontinental nuclear systems and, with the full deployment of US INF, there will be a crude INF parity. The difficulty of assessing which side is stronger is demonstrated by examining the US–Soviet strategic nuclear balance. There is an asymmetry in land-based, sea-based and bomber systems, and, as Table 1 shows, while the US is 'stronger' in warheads, the Soviet Union has more delivery systems. The net political effect of such 'strengths' and 'weaknesses' is negligible. What is important is that neither side has any

Table 1   US–Soviet strategic (intercontinental) nuclear balance, 1984

| | US | | Soviet Union | |
	warheads	delivery systems	warheads	delivery systems
ICBM	2,145	1,045	6,273	1,398
SLBM	5,152	568	2,317	941
Long-range bombers	2,368	241	290	145
Totals	9,665	1,854	8,880	2,484

Figures from Lodgaard, S. and Blackaby, F. (1984) 'Nuclear Weapons', in Stockholm International Peace Research Institute, *The Arms Race and Arms Control* (1984), London and Philadelphia, Taylor and Francis, pp. 22, 25.

clear-cut military advantage, and each realizes that it could not use its nuclear military power in any unilateral fashion to pursue a political end, because the consequences would be incalculable. Such parity seems likely to continue until at least the end of this century. This does not mean to say that efforts at arms control ought to be abandoned. While there is parity and balance, that parity must be protected and the balance improved. Ideally, parity should continue, but at lower warhead and delivery systems totals. With fewer systems there is less chance of accidents and a greater prospect of more prudent use in the event of conflict. It is also cheaper to procure fewer systems, but to fall below a certain minimum level of warheads could endanger deterrence by depriving the superpowers of the capability to threaten assured destruction. At lower levels but above minimum requirements, balance could be improved and stability enhanced by phasing out the more vulnerable systems, which present tempting targets for first strikes and the most accurate systems that can fulfil first strike roles. Such weaknesses and strengths come together in land-based ICBMs. In this regard, a major problem for East–West arms control is the asymmetry of the superpower arsenals. Such an arms control model as described above would mean a much greater cut in the Soviet land-based ICBM force than in that of the United States.

Destabilization of the nuclear balance would occur if there were any major unilateral defensive breakthroughs, especially in the fields of BMD and ASW (anti-submarine warfare). BMD deployment is presently limited by the ABM Treaty of 1972 and its 1974 amendment, whereby each superpower is limited to one ABM system each. The treaty is reviewed every five years, and sometimes there are dark hints in Washington about abrogating it, but to do so would be a major defeat for those who support balanced, symmetrical arms control and pin their hopes for continued East–West peace on mutual vulnerability. However, even if a BMD arms race began with a vengeance, there seems to be a consensus amongst the scientific community in the West that affordable, feasible blanket BMD is most unlikely for decades to come.[1] At the very most, in perhaps ten years, there may be some point BMD being deployed to protect ICBM silos and command facilities.

Effective ASW against deep-diving SSBNs with ever longer ranges is reckoned to be as unlikely as effective blanket BMD, once missiles are launched. In the strategic and defence studies community there is little indication of any significant technological breakthrough in ASW. The continuing strong SSBN construction programmes of the United States, the Soviet Union, Britain and France support this view.

At the conventional military level of the bloc balance in Europe, as long as NATO steadily modernizes its conventional forces and cautiously adapts its military tactics to suit new circumstances, there is little need for acute alarm. Some bureaucrats, soldiers and politicians in the defence field are prone to exaggerate NATO's weaknesses and the Warsaw Pact's strengths. This should not be surprising, as it is the job of such professionals to plan for the worst. But if one assumes a few days' warning time (not an unreasonable expectation given modern and traditional means of intelligence), if one counts French forces and West German reserve forces in the balance of manpower, and if one accepts that some benefit may be derived from being the defender and fighting on familiar territory, then even the static bean-count approach to assessing the conventional military balance does not condemn the West to humiliating defeat within seventy-two or ninety-six hours. Indeed, it would be totally unrealistic to expect that the Warsaw Pact could organize its forces for a massive attack on West Europe in absolute secrecy, that their offensive and reinforcements strategies would go like clockwork, or that the East European Warsaw Pact armies would be equally enthusiastic for battle while the NATO democracies fell into disarray at the first sign of hostile intentions.[2] The Warsaw Pact does present a picture of a most formidable war-fighting machine, seemingly in a state of perpetual modernization. However, NATO's long-term defence improvement programme (LTDP) has led to a modernization and upgrading of conventional forces and infrastructure, with the objectives of keeping pace with Warsaw Pact developments and also decreasing reliance on BNW (battlefield nuclear weapons).[3] Increasingly, BNW, rather than the strategic missile systems, are seen to be the major threat to security and conflict limitation in the event of hostilities. As the first rung on the ladder of nuclear escalation is the early resort to BNW, then tactics at this threshold between conventional and nuclear war are crucial.

At present there is considerable debate in military and academic circles over the future conventional and tactical direction of deterrence and defence in Europe. How much should NATO depend on modern computerized, micro-chip, conventional defence technology? Should NATO conventional force be organized to fight the war on the inner German border and defeat the front echelons of the Soviet forces, or should the major effort be directed towards 'striking deep' at the rear, reinforcing echelons of the Warsaw Pact? Should NATO forces contemplate counter-offensives which could take land forces over the IGB into Warsaw Pact territory? These are questions exercising participants in the debate over NATO's conventional and battlefield nuclear future.[4] A common objective is to raise the nuclear threshold as high as possible, but most of the participants in the debate do not support dispensing with the nuclear threshold altogether. While there are strong arguments supporting a 'no first use' doctrine,[5] there are even more compelling arguments for retaining the threat of the prospect of first use of nuclear weapons during a conflict already under way.[6] While there is consensus that the early resort to first use of nuclear weapons should be avoided, the thrust of the arguments of those who support first use is that for a defensive alliance to deny itself possible recourse to any weapon in the event of aggression is to weaken deterrence and make such aggression less unlikely. Furthermore, a declaration of no first use could have dire political consequences for NATO. It could reduce the confidence of the Federal Republic in the total commitment of its NATO partners to its defence.

Analyses of the military balance in Europe abound: the best pay heed to political, economic and social as well as military and strategic factors in assessing the balance.[7] For instance, it is usually assumed that any war in central Europe will be a short war. The same assumptions were made in 1914 and 1939. It could transpire that any future European war could be a long, stop–start war of attrition. That being the case the economic and social strengths of the democracies would be a most positive factor in their favour. Most of these mainstream analyses are not unduly pessimistic in either the short or the long term, provided that NATO remains alert, force levels are sustained, modernization continues and weaknesses are identified and tackled. The comments of the IISS in London in 1984 are a fair reflection of such opinion:

Because of the presence in the equation of so many unknown and unknowable factors, one cannot necessarily conclude that NATO would suffer defeat in war, nor that the Warsaw Pact would see its advantage as being sufficient to risk an attack, but one can conclude that there is still sufficient danger in the trend to require remedies in the Western Alliance, particularly as manpower shortage becomes a problem by the end of the 1980s.

Our conclusion remains that the conventional overall balance is still such as to make general military aggression a highly risky undertaking. Though tactical redeployments could certainly provide a local advantage in numbers sufficient to allow an attacker to believe that he might achieve limited tactical successes in some exposed areas, there would still appear to be insufficient overall strength to guarantee victory. The consequences for an attacker would

still be somewhat unpredictable, and the risks – particularly of nuclear escalation – incalculable.[8]

The major current military–strategic threat to European
security is a conceptual one, not a practical, actual military
imbalance at any level. Arguments in support of strategic
defence, particularly BMD, give succour to the contemporary
alarmist criticisms of deterrence theory. Support for the expendi-
ture of billions of dollars on research and development in pursuit
of a new strategic concept to replace the one which has served the
West for the past thirty years demands that the present strategy
be criticized as inadequate. As a result, those on the far left of the
political spectrum in the West who have been arguing that
deterrence is immoral, illogical, unstable and bound to lead to
catastrophe some day are deriving a considerable degree of
support from the Republican administration in Washington and
from some sectors of the American military–industrial complex.
For most of the postwar era the electorates of the West have
accepted that deterrence was a viable strategic doctrine for
their defence. It seems likely that SDI will be unable to deliver
anything approaching invulnerability to nuclear attack. It had
never been intended that it would replace conventional deterrence and defence. Indeed, it could be argued that effective BMD
for both sides makes resort to conventional war a less unattractive policy option. The West's defence will continue to rely on
deterrence-based strategic doctrine. But, given the buffeting to
which deterrence has been subjected from both extremes of the
Western political spectrum in recent years, is it possible to expect
public confidence in deterrence to continue as before?

It is particularly ironic that deterrence is under such attack in
an era when the overall East–West military balance has never
been so stable. Both East and West have more than sufficient
forces to inflict assured destruction, even after suffering a first
strike. Also, both sides retain the capabilities for graduated
response at various levels of threat, and neither is faced by an
'all or nothing' dilemma in the event of aggression by the
other side. However, it is the very stability of current East–West
relations which may account for the enthusiasm for strategic
defence in many political circles in the West, especially in the

Republican Party. Many American politicians have found it difficult to reconcile themselves to the loss of United States military superiority; crude military equality with the Soviet Union is deemed unacceptable, and the search is on for ways to regain that US superiority. Deterrence-based strategies will continue to form the foundations for the defence of West Europe at conventional and nuclear level up to the beginning of the next century and beyond. The superpower strategic nuclear balance will remain rooted in the reality of mutual assured destruction, even though the route to that undesirable outcome could be somewhat impeded by the developments in BMD. Indeed, one paradox of successful BMD research leading to the defence of counter-force targets will be to increase the value of societal targets for the purposes of retaliation and retribution.

In recent years it has been fashionable to identify threats to West European security arising outside the NATO area. These threats are seen to challenge Western political influence or access to markets and vital minerals and raw materials. Some influential voices have called for an enlargement of the NATO area, to incorporate parts of the developing world which are of political, strategic and economic importance to the West.[9] This alarm over the perceived strategic encirclement of the West, and the possible denial of access to raw materials and markets, has been based, amongst other things, on the experience of the brief Arab oil embargo of 1973, the use of Cuban troops in Africa in the 1970s, the fall of South Vietnam in 1975, the collapse of the administration of the Shah in Iran, the Soviet invasion of Afghanistan, and the overthrow of the Somoza regime in Nicaragua by an indigenous revolutionary movement with socialist objectives. The United States has been particularly alarmed, and has established the Rapid Deployment Force (RDF) to tackle any direct military threat to US interests in the Gulf in particular, or in other vital parts of the developing world. Pressure has been put on the Europeans to assist; in particular, the British government has responded by establishing a limited airborne interventionary force of brigade strength. This decision was taken before the Falklands War of 1982 and, although the Falklands War was not the sort of out-of-area operation envisaged for the use of such a force, the success of that instance of power projection provided an impetus to the revival of British interventionary forces. France also has a large airborne interventionary force, used on a number of occasions to protect French interests in Francophone Africa.

NATO, however, has not acted as an alliance in this field, for there is a great reluctance to countenance the expansion of its responsibility. There is an acute awareness that an alliance of sixteen nations would not be the best vehicle to manage risky interventions in volatile parts of the world in pursuit of what would probably be controversial objectives. In any case, there is no consensus in NATO that Western interests in the developing world are under threat. There are very few raw materials on which West Europe is dependent, which come from one source, that cannot be substituted or produced synthetically, or of which short-term crisis of supply could not be averted by prudent stockpiling.[10] Even with the case of oil, such has been the success of the Western oil conservation efforts and diversification of sources that there is now an international oil glut. When radical regimes do emerge in states with vital raw materials, the record is that they wish to sustain trade with the West. The attractions of Western currency, technology and credit are such that countries such as Libya, Iran, Angola, Mozambique and Zimbabwe are desperate for Western custom, and appear to have no desire to cut off trade with the West for political purposes, regardless of the rhetoric of their leaders. States may be identified in official circles as client states of the Soviet Union, but invariably Soviet political control is weak and does not extend to trading relations. Unless Western hostility offers no alternative, most developing world states with popular revolutionary governments do not fall under immutable Soviet control:

Cold War experience teaches that the Soviets do not expand via national revolution, but by the force of the Soviet army. Time and again, Soviet influence has proven ephemeral wherever its army was not introduced, even where Soviet 'proxies' won control. The notion that Third World leftists are loyal Soviet minions seldom proves correct, except when American policies help make it true, as with Vietnam, Cuba, Nicaragua, and earlier with China.[11]

Some Western interventionary forces are required as a deterrent to possible Soviet long-range military adventurism. In this regard US power projection forces, if necessary with British and French forces giving moral support, are more than adequate to any potential challenge. US power projection capabilities far exceed those of the Soviet Union. Sea and air power are essential elements in long-range power projection: by 1990 the United States will have fifteen aircraft carrier task groups and the Soviet Union will perhaps have three or four. The United States Marine Corps is 200,000 strong, the Soviet Marine Corps about 16,000. If one casts a glance at the Western, particularly American, bases and alliances throughout the developing world, then the balance of political and military advantage is seen to weigh heavily in the favour of the West. Even in areas contiguous to the Soviet Union, for instance Iran, the Soviet Union encounters vast logistical problems, and certainly could not launch a major surprise attack in a drive for the Gulf oil fields. Such would be the diversion of resources from other fronts and the build-up of material that Soviet intentions would be obvious to all.

In the postwar era it cannot be argued that the Soviet Union has had outstanding military and political success in the developing world. The only instance of the direct use of Soviet military force outside East Europe has been the occupation of Afghanistan since 1979. Peaceful control of the country has still to be achieved, and the authority of the Soviet-backed regime seems to hold sway only in the major cities during daylight hours, and periodically in selected rural areas. As an illustration of the efficacy of Soviet power projection capabilities, the Afghanistan experience is not encouraging for the Soviet Union. Although it has established a number of close allies, specifically Cuba, Vietnam, Ethiopia, the People's Democratic Republic of Yemen and perhaps Syria, and exercises greater political influence than the West in Angola, Libya, Mozambique, Nicaragua and North Korea, the Soviet Union has 'lost' the PRC, Egypt, Indonesia, Sudan, Somalia and Iraq. The prospects for Soviet foreign policy in the developing world up to the end of the century are not especially bright. On the other hand, for NATO to extend its geographical area south of the Tropic of Cancer could be very counter-productive, and would be seen by the developing world as arrogant and imperialistic. There is little likelihood of harmony within NATO if, in such circumstances, the United States were to call for NATO intervention in Central America in response to a perceived Communist threat, or intervention in the Gulf to prop up a conservative pro-American regime. There is little need for NATO to extend its area of responsibility, and it would be to the detriment of the Alliance to do so.[12] There is also little likelihood that it will happen.

In West Europe the political bases underpinning security arrangements are sound. Twenty years ago NATO weathered well the withdrawal of France from the integrated military structure of the Alliance (though not from the Alliance itself). Since 1967 there has been no shock to the system of a similar scale. The paradox of the French withdrawal from NATO's integrated military structure is that it was not in order to facilitate a pacifist or neutralist policy. De Gaulle, and all his successors as president of the Fifth Republic, have supported a strong defence policy, with a very robust nuclear component. While not always agreeing with the practice of Alliance policy, and bristling against the Anglo-Saxon dominance in decision-making, French governments have been supportive of the concept of the Atlantic Alliance and the United States' commitment to West European security. The government of President Mitterrand, a socialist, has been unwaveringly committed to INF modernization, and is pursuing an ambitious programme of modernization of French nuclear and conventional forces.[13]

Recent years have witnessed a number of intramural NATO disputes over how best to respond to a number of divisive items on the Alliance agenda, such as developments in Poland, Soviet foreign policy outside the NATO area, arms control, economic policy towards the East, and burden-sharing within the Alliance. Yet, despite harsh words, imprudent gestures and some unilateral actions, the integrity of NATO as a nuclear military alliance has not been under serious threat. It has not been on the verge of disintegration, such as would be occasioned by the complete withdrawal of the United States, or Britain, or the Federal Republic. Nevertheless, major intramural problems loom ahead. A primary irritant to West–West relations will be the future of arms control, and the extra complicating factor of the introduction of defensive systems by one side into negotiations which, for more than ten years, have been about offensive systems. The Gorbachev regime in Moscow looks as if it may adopt a more conciliatory approach to West Europe in an effort to detach West European support from the United States' position on arms control. The US record in this area in the years of the Reagan presidency has not been encouraging for West Europeans, and the commitment to arms control as an instrument for enhancing stable security rather than competing with the Soviet Union is perceived to be low. Some imaginative arms control proposals derived from realistic assessments of the strategic nuclear balance, together with some record of practical achievement, would go a long way towards reassuring West European governments that Washington's attitude to arms control in the 1980s is not actually detrimental to European security.

Another major political problem is likely to be that of burden-sharing for conventional defence. This is not a new problem for NATO. But the demands put on the defence budgets of the members by the introduction of some, or a lot, of the emerging technology (ET) of defence will be such that the Alliance will again experience strain over burden-sharing. A further facet of this issue is that while the United States may claim to be bearing a disproportionate share of the NATO defence burden – an argument which the West Europeans do not accept – a disproportionate amount of the ET military hardware which NATO will be encouraged to buy will be produced in the United States. At the end of the day such will be the pressure on scarce defence resources that a radical restructuring of member states' commitments and responsibilities, and military tactics, may be forced upon the Alliance rather than adopted through choice.[14] However, the Alliance will survive. The Warsaw Pact will continue to be perceived to pose a considerable political and military threat to which NATO is the most prudent and cost-effective response. It seems most unlikely that NATO, in the remainder of this century, will undergo anything similar to the traumatic events which the Communist bloc experienced with the Sino-Soviet split.

While intramural problems will persist for NATO, it seems

likely that only events in East Europe could hasten the untimely demise of the Western half of the European bloc system. If the Soviet grip on East Europe could be so loosened that the Soviet Union felt unable to control East Europe any longer, and retreated behind the 1945 Soviet borders, the overt Soviet threat to West Europe would then diminish to such an extent that NATO's importance as a security device would decline, and the Alliance would fade into history. This scenario is highly unlikely: it would take a radical change in Soviet domestic politics, coupled with a severe Soviet economic crisis, for it to occur. For strategic and economic reasons East Europe will continue to be the area of most vital interest to the Soviet Union, next to homeland defence, for many years ahead. The 'loss' of East Europe would reduce the Soviet Union to a regional great power deprived of its vital trading partners, raise the spectre of a reunified Germany, and bring American and German political and economic influence up to the banks of the Vistula. Major threats to Soviet hegemony in East Europe arising from external or internal sources will continue to justify, in Soviet eyes, the use of coercion. The Soviet Union is determined to sustain its half of the bloc system. This is *the* major problem for European security in the next ten to twenty years, in comparison with which the bickering in NATO over burden-sharing pales into insignificance.

It is not inconceivable that an intramural Warsaw Pact crisis, involving the use of armed force, especially in the northern tier states of Poland, the German Democratic Republic, Czechoslovakia and Hungary, could spill over the Iron Curtain, in a political or military fashion, and inveigle individual NATO states or the Alliance as a whole. Such a scenario is pessimistic, but all is not well in the Warsaw Pact. There is a severe problem of legitimacy for the regimes in East Europe, to be found throughout all classes of East European society, from the intelligentsia in the East German and Hungarian universities to industrial workers in the Czechoslovakian machine-tool factories and the crane drivers of the Polish dockyards.[15] This crisis of legitimacy for the ruling regimes is particularly acute amongst the younger generations. The cloak of legitimacy provided by Marxism–Leninism is seen to be threadbare, as state inefficiency and corruption are obvious to all and economic aspirations are consistently dashed. The economic exception to the rule in recent years has been Hungary, but this is as a result of, in East European terms, a most adventurous economic management system.

Even in the field of security, the system is seen to be failing the people. The emplacement of Soviet INF with nuclear warheads throughout East Europe, as a response to NATO INF deployments, has raised considerable doubts in the minds of East European governments and peoples as to the quality of the security provided by the Soviet-dominated Warsaw Pact. The Warsaw Pact has experienced its own intra-mural crisis over INF, and alliance problems on this issue have not been confined to NATO.[16] The mid 1980s saw an unprecedented assertion of political independence by some leading East European states, and virtual political debate between the state organs of fellow Warsaw Pact members, with the German Democratic Republic and Hungary supporting a particular view strongly criticized by the Soviet Union and Czechoslovakia.[17] The immediate issue at stake was the visit by the East German leader, Honecker, to the Federal Republic, the first time such a visit would ever have taken place. It was to have occurred in the midst of an aggressive Soviet political campaign against the West for deploying INF in West Europe, but eventually public Soviet pressure inhibited the visit, and it was cancelled. However, a short while later a point was made about official East European unease over the whole European arms control problem by the visit of Honecker to Italy, a country where INF were to be deployed.

This is not to suggest that the Communist regimes in East Europe are in sympathy with popular discontent and uneasy with the system as it stands. But the INF issue, on the eastern side of the Iron Curtain, has added fuel to the fire of political and economic discontent manifested by Charter 77 in Czechoslovakia, Solidarity in Poland, the unofficial peace movement in the German Democratic Republic, and the general resurgence of religion and nationalism as 'alternative ideologies'.[18] Such developments, which are essentially of human derivation and hence less liable to control and curtailment, seem deep-rooted in East European society. In the longer term it appears inevitable that there will be some kind of gradual change in Soviet–East European relations and within East European societies of an order not likely to be encountered in West Europe. If there is not gradual change then there could be an explosion, or a series of explosions, of political conflict which could have dire consequences for all Europe. West Europe may have economic and social problems, but the actual legitimacy of the state system and the security arrangements are not held in question as they are in many parts of East Europe. For better or worse, these changes in East Europe will affect West European security. What should the West do?

East Europe is a volatile area, with many nationalist, political and economic rivalries. For European stability it is best that a regional great power should exert influence and control such rivalries, but to do so to such an extent that it stifles legitimate national self-expression clearly cannot continue indefinitely. If Soviet control and Communist Party dominance are to be diluted, but not removed, then the West should assist in the gradual management of these new developments – but cautiously. While delighted to see liberalization in East Europe, the West should not encourage the rejection of Soviet hegemony, nor should it challenge Soviet political and military influence in the region. The heavy-handed encouragement of East European dissident movements or 'renegade' governments will do little good to the slow process of peaceful accommodation to change, and fuel Soviet anxieties. Indeed, in the event of a fading-away of the bloc system in Europe, it is in the interests of European security that considerable Soviet influence remain in East Europe, so long as it is not antithetical to legitimate Western interests. Again, this is perhaps expecting too much of the Soviet Union unless there are radical domestic political changes, but alternative scenarios of disruption and conflict in East Europe and heightened Soviet paranoia are less attractive to contemplate. The East European question is a long-term issue, but it is one of immense political importance for the West. It is worthy of major attention, and delicate diplomacy, now.

Trade and economic relations within the blocs and between them have traditionally been treated apart from security relations.[19] There have been exceptions to this rule, but

generally economic matters are dealt with by different depart-
ments in the national bureaucracies, and by people with different
expertise from those in the security field. When this has not been
the case, then the 'linkage' between economic and security issues
has been managed at the highest level. However, the radically
changing international economic environment over the past
twenty years has elevated many middle-range economic matters
– for instance, the export of subsidized steel from West Europe to
the United States – to issues of high policy-making. Also, in the
minds of the general public and many legislators, adverse trade
balances in West–West trade which favour West Europe are
contrasted with the perceived imbalance in defence contributions
to NATO, where the United States appears to be subsidising
West European security.

A further West–West economic problem is that of trade with
the East. What sort of goods should be exported to the East, what
sort of business ought to be conducted with the East, and in what
way and to what extent should the economic instrument be used
to punish or persuade the East? These are questions which have
exercised Western policy-makers in recent years. The West
Europeans tend to see trade with the East as a foundation for
good East–West relations and as an ameliorative, 'business-as-
usual' process during periods of East–West political and military
tension. Across the North Atlantic the view tends to be that
control of trade may be used to demonstrate displeasure with the
East's actions or even to attempt to change the policies of
adversaries. The intra-Alliance disputes in the early 1980s over
the building of the Soviet gas pipeline to West Europe and the
purchase of Soviet gas by some West European NATO states,
and the use of trade sanctions against Poland by the West
following the military coup in December 1981, illustrate the
growing linkage between politics and economics at the highest
levels. This is unlikely to diminish as the century draws to a
close.

Such problems in the West will not go away as trade
competition intensifies and the cost and complexity of defence
increase. To date such problems have been managed and, while
crisis will continue, it is encouraging that Western leaders seem
able to identify a higher common security interest that should not

be undermined by economic bickering. One optimistic view holds that

> it would be useful for both policy-makers and commentators simply to recognise that there will be occasional disputes over economic issues and that those will strain Alliance co-operation across the board. In some instances the United States and her allies ought to try to agree to disagree, to recognise that the best they can do is limit the damage. If my conclusion is correct – if economic disputes and their spill-over in other Alliance arrangements will be greater in the future but not dramatically so – the damage should be manageable. At least that should be so long as there is no serious economic shock.[20]

Nor are economic tensions with political implications confined to the West. As the East European economies have recovered in the postwar era, the balance of trade and the nature of the trade between the Soviet Union and its East European CMEA partners have been a source of considerable friction. For reasons of consumer demand, tradition, economic management and geography, many of the national economies in the East make uneasy bedfellows with their CMEA neighbours, and there are stark contrasts in productivity and in living standards throughout the Eastern bloc. The main pattern of trade in the CMEA is that the Soviet Union exchanges fuel and raw materials for East European manufactured goods. After a lull in the early 1980s East European countries are again borrowing heavily from Western banks, and growth rates in East Europe are again picking up. Trade and economic relations are more unpredictable even than developments in international politics. What is predictable is that economic factors will gain in political significance within the blocs in both East and West, and between the blocs.

Europe is not on the brink of war. Within the blocs there is a slow process of gradual change, and there are many prominent, sensitive issues between the blocs. Between the blocs there remains a deep ideological divide, which will continue until there are radical political changes in the East or in the West. Such radical political change looks most unlikely, so the ideological

divide will remain a fact of life for international society. It is, of
course, ideological differences which lie at the heart of East–West
competition as we know it. Arms control talks and multilateral
security conferences are worthy exercises, and ought to be
pursued realistically and urgently; more stable nuclear and
conventional arms balances at lower levels are possible, and
would enhance security for everyone. But, dismantling the
alliance blocs and real disarmament are impossible in the
absence of political trust, and neither side is prepared to trust the
other in the face of long-held and deeply rooted ideological
differences. Both sides can point to recent history for reasons why
they should not trust their perceived adversaries.

As a result, two blocs have developed in Europe whose
leaderships, though not always the peoples, are fundamentally
distrustful of each other. Over the past forty years political and
strategic competition has always been present, and has often
reached crisis proportions. Yet competition has been controlled,
and conflict between the blocs in Europe avoided. The crucial
factor inhibiting conflict has been the existence of nuclear
weapons. Some people may regret that such weapons were ever
developed. But they cannot be disinvented. Strategies have been
devised for the control and exercise of the nuclear power that
nuclear weapons deliver. These strategies are not perfect but, to
date, it is clear that the costs of nuclear conflict have been a
major influence on decision-makers when considering the use of
military force to protect or pursue political objectives in Europe.
Given the vulnerabilities of modern societies, caution has been
the order of the day in Europe. Both superpowers are present in
the heart of the continent, and in the event of war between East
and West they could not avoid conflict with each other.
Paradoxically, this makes war less likely in this most heavily
armed area of the globe.

A blind conviction in the inevitability and virtues of wholesale
unilateral or multilateral disarmament, or hopes that the
dismantling of the alliance blocs will return Europe to a mythical
Edwardian system of sovereign nation-states, or faith that one's
political creed is so superior that it will eventually triumph if
allowed unfettered competition against the adversary, fly in the
face of the realities of the modern European world. Understand-

ing European security requires grasping and facing up to realities: the realities of ideological division, of the presence of nuclear weapons and the vulnerabilities of advanced societies, and of the geopolitical division of Europe into two hostile blocs with a smattering of neutrals on the periphery. Most leaders in both East and West have faced up to these realities in the postwar era. While advancing the interests of their own societies, these leaders have attempted realistic accommodation – political, military and economic – with the other side, conscious that any negotiated outcomes between very different political creeds with asymmetrical geostrategic perspectives are bound by their very nature to be imperfect. What is clear is that nearly all the decision-makers have been fully aware of the nuclear world in which they are operating, aware that failure to reach some accommodation and to address realities could mean catastrophe for all.

Notes

CHAPTER 1 FORTY YEARS OF SECURITY

1   See Segal, G., Moreton, E., Freedman, L. and Baylis, J. (1983) *Nuclear War and Nuclear Peace*, London, Macmillan, p. 113.

2   Foot, P. (1983) *The Protesters*, Centre Piece 14, Aberdeen, Centre for Defence Studies, p. 32.

3   Moisi, D. (1983) 'Domestic Priorities and the Demands of Alliance: A European Perspective', *Defence and Consensus: The Domestic Aspects of Western Security Part III*, Adelphi Paper 184, London, International Institute for Strategic Studies (IISS), p. 14.

4   de Leon, P. (1983) 'Freeze: The Literature of the Nuclear Weapons Debate', *Journal of Conflict Resolution*, Vol. 27, No. 1, March 1983, p. 182.

5   Pym, F. (1982) 'Defense in Democracies', *International Security*, Vol. 7, No. 1, Spring 1982, p. 41.

6   See Freedman, L. (1982a) 'Limited War, Unlimited Protest', *Orbis*, Vol. 26, No. 1, Spring 1982, p. 89.

7   See van Voorst, L. Bruce (1982) 'The Critical Masses', *Foreign Policy 48*, Fall 1982, p. 83.

8   Ibid., p. 89. The complete resolution is reprinted in de Leon (1983), p. 183.

9   See Griffith, W.E. (1982) 'Bonn and Washington: From Deterioration to Crisis?', *Orbis*, Vol. 26, No 1, Spring 1982, p. 130; and '139 in Congress Urge Nuclear Arms Freeze by US and Moscow', *New York Times*, 11 March, 1982, p.A1.

10 Ibid., p. 131.

11 See van Voorst (1982), pp. 86–87.

12 Cited in van Voorst, L. Bruce (1983) 'The Churches and Nuclear Deterrence', *Foreign Affairs*, Vol. 61, No 4, Spring 1983, p. 846.

13 See Boutwell, J. (1983) 'Politics and the Peace Movement in West Germany' *International Security*, Vol. 7, No. 4, Spring 1983, p. 73.

14 For instance, see Smart, I. (1977) 'Beyond Polaris', *International Affairs*, Vol. 53, No. 4, October 1977; Nailor, P. and Alford, J. (1980), *The Future of Britain's Deterrent Force*, Adelphi Paper 156, London, IISS; and *The Future United Kingdom Strategic Nuclear Deterrent Force* (1980), Defence Open Government Document 80/23, London, Ministry of Defence, July 1980.

15 Treverton, G. (1981) *Nuclear Weapons in Europe*, Adelphi Paper 168, London, IISS, p. 6.

16 See Boutwell (1983) p. 89, fn. 35.

17 Freedman, L. (1982) 'NATO Myths', *Foreign Policy 45*, Winter 1981/82, p. 48.

18 van Voorst (1982), p. 84.

19 *International Herald Tribune*, 21 October 1981, cited in Freedman, L. (1982a) p. 98, fn. 12.

20 Roberts, A. (1983) 'The Critique of Nuclear Deterrence', *Defence and Consensus: The Domestic Aspects of Western Security Part II*, Adelphi Paper 183, London, IISS, pp. 9–10.

21 Kaagan, L. (1983) 'Public Opinion and the Defence Effort: Trends and Lessons', *Defence and Consensus: The Domestic Aspects of Western Security Part I*, Adelphi Paper 182, London, IISS, p. 23.

22 See Griffith, W.E. (1982), p. 120.

23 See *The Military Balance 1984–85* (1984), London, IISS.

24 Halperin, M. (1982) 'NATO and the TNF Controversy: Threats to the Alliance', *Orbis*, Vol. 26, No 1, Spring 1982, p. 106.

CHAPTER 2   THE IDEOLOGICAL CONFLICT

1 See Clemens, D.S. (1972) *YALTA*, London, Oxford University Press, p. 75.

2 See Mastny, V. (1979) *Russia's Road to the Cold War*, New York, Columbia University Press, pp. 72–77; Nogee, J.L. and Donaldson, R.H. (1981) *Soviet Foreign Policy Since World War II*, New York, Pergamon Press, pp. 46–48; and Ulam, A.B. (1974) *Expansion and Coexistence*, New York, Praeger, p. 338.

3 See Ulam (1974), p. 276.

4 See Halle, L.J. (1967) *The Cold War As History*, London, Chatto and Windus, p. 57.

5 De Porte, A.W. (1979) *Europe Between the Superpowers*, New Haven and London, Yale University Press, p. 94, and Clemens (1972), Chap. 5.

6   Clemens (1972), p. 176.
7   See Mastny (1979), pp. 183–186, and Ulam (1974), pp. 361–363.
8   Ulam (1974), p. 364.
9   See Clemens (1972), p. 303.
10 Nogee and Donaldson (1981), p. 51, and Ulam (1974), pp. 378–380.
11 Halle (1967), p. 65.
12 See Grosser, A. (1980) *The Western Alliance*, London, Macmillan, pp. 59–62.
13 For an assessment of the 'universalist' versus 'balance of power/spheres of influence' concepts of international security, see Schlesinger Jr., A. 'Origins of the Cold War', in Hoffmann, E.P. and Fleron, F.J. (eds) (1980) *The Conduct of Soviet Foreign Policy*, New York, Aldine, pp. 228–254.
14 See Yergin, D. (1980) *The Shattered Peace*, Harmondsworth, Penguin, p. 324, and Ulam (1974), p. 436.
15 For instance, see Carew Hunt, R.N. et al. 'Ideology and Power Priorities: A Symposium', in Hoffmann and Fleron (1980), Chap. 7.
16 See Schlesinger in Hoffman and Fleron (1980), p. 251.
17 For the scale of Soviet losses between 1941 and 1945, and the symbolic and practical significance of reparations, see Yergin (1980), pp. 64–65.
18 Ibid., pp. 95–97 and pp. 298–300.
19 See De Porte (1979), p. 145.
20 Morgan, R. (1972) *West European Politics since 1945*, London, Batsford, p. 51.
21 On Marshall's perspective in 1946, see Yergin (1980), pp. 299–300.
22 Nogee and Donaldson (1981), pp. 68–69.
23 Aron, R. (1965) *The Century of Total War*, Boston, Beacon Press, p. 49.
24 Thomson, D. (1967) *Europe Since Napoleon*, Harmondsworth, Penguin, p. 35.
25 Bond, B. (1984) *War and Society in Europe 1870–1970*, London, Fontana, p. 195.
26 Thomson (1967), p. 549.
27 Aron (1965), p. 28.
28 See Watt, D.C. (1967) *A History of the World in the Twentieth Century*, London, Pan, pp. 246–249.
29 Aron (1965), p. 15.
30 Quoted in Rees, D. (1971) *The Age of Containment*, London, Macmillan, p. 21.

31 See Yergin (1980), p. 275.
32 Ambrose, S.E. (1973) *Rise to Globalism*, Harmondsworth, Penguin, pp. 149–150.
33 Rees (1971), pp. 21–23.
34 See Yergin (1980), p. 283.
35 Kennan, G. (1951) 'The Sources of Soviet Conduct', *American Diplomacy 1900–1950*, New York, Mentor, p. 96 and p. 99, reprinted from *Foreign Affairs*, Vol. 25, No. 4 (July 1947), pp. 566–582.
36 Ibid., p. 99.
37 See Gaddis, J.L. (1982) *Strategies of Containment*, Oxford, Oxford University Press, pp. 27–51.
38 Kennan, G. (1967) *Memoirs 1925–1950*, Boston, Little, Brown and Co., pp. 355–363.
39 Ambrose (1973), p. 167.
40 Ibid., p. 149.
41 See Gaddis (1982), pp. 19–21.
42 De Porte, (1979)p. 128.
43 Ibid.
44 Bond (1984), p. 206.
45 For details of the Hungarian uprising see Ulam (1974), pp. 595–598.
46 Spanier, J. (1972) *American Foreign Policy Since World War II*, London, Nelson, p. 111.
47 Statement of John F. Kennedy, 28 August 1962, reported in the *New York Times*, 29 August 1962, quoted in Barnet, R.J. (1972) *Intervention and Revolution*, London, Paladin, pp. 24–25.
48 Address by Lyndon Johnson, 12 February 1965, reported in *New York Times*, 13 February 1965, quoted in Barnet (1972), p. 24.
49 See Kissinger, H. (1979) *The White House Years*, London, Weidenfeld and Nicolson and Michael Joseph, pp. 221–225.
50 See Edmonds, R. (1977) *Soviet Foreign Policy 1962–1973*, London, Oxford University Press, p. 4.
51 See Wolfe, T.W. (1970) *Soviet Power and Europe 1945–1970*, Baltimore, Johns Hopkins Press, p. 25 and p. 54.
52 See Nogee and Donaldson (1981), pp. 92–93.
53 See Dinerstein, H. (1962) *War and the Soviet Union*, New York, Frederick A. Praeger, pp. 15–23.
54 Nogee and Donaldson (1981), p. 27.
55 Khrushchev's report to the 20th CPSU Congress, 1956, quoted in Nogee and Donaldson (1981), pp. 28–29 and p. 30.
56 Garthoff, R. (1971) *Soviet Military Policy*, London, Faber, pp. 24–28.
57 Ibid., p. 90.

58   See Edmonds (1977), p. 2.
59   Horelick, A.L. and Rush, M. (1966) *Strategic Power and Soviet Foreign Policy*, Chicago, University of Chicago Press, p. 119.
60   See Wolfe (1970), p. 256, and Edmonds (1977), p. 36.
61   Quoted in Edmonds (1977), p. 3.
62   Hoffmann and Fleron (1980), p. 294.
63   Edmonds (1977), p. 127.
64   Nogee and Donaldson (1981), p. 238.
65   Quoted in Bell, C. (1977) *The Diplomacy of Détente*, London, Martin Robertson, p. 4.
66   Ibid., pp. 1-2.
67   See Steele, J. (1983) *World Power*, London, Michael Joseph, pp. 50–51.
68   See Wolfe (1970), pp. 101–108.
69   Steele (1983), p. 51.
70   Brown, S. (1983) *The Faces of Power*, New York, Columbia University Press, p. 335.
71   See Bell (1977), p. 3.
72   See Kissinger (1979), pp. 132–133.
73   Gaddis (1982), p. 289.
74   For commentary on, and texts of, the United States–Soviet Union bilateral agreements from May 1972, see Timberlake, C. (1978) *Détente: A Documentary Record*, London, Praeger.
75   See Brown, S. (1979) *The Crises of Power*, New York, Columbia University Press, p. 15.
76   See Mandelbaum, M. (1979) *The Nuclear Question*, Cambridge, Cambridge University Press, p. 200.
77   See Pipes, R. (1976) 'Détente: Moscow's view', in Pipes, R. (ed.) *Soviet Strategy in Europe*, New York, Crane, Russak and Co., p. 23.
78   See Nogee and Donaldson (1981), p. 251.
79   Henry Kissinger press conference, 25 October 1973, quoted in Edmonds (1977), p. 168.

CHAPTER 3   THE NUCLEAR ENVIRONMENT

1   Mandelbaum, M. (1981) *The Nuclear Revolution*, Cambridge, Cambridge University Press, p. 210.
2   Wolfe, T.W. (1970) *Soviet Power and Europe 1945–1970*, Baltimore, Johns Hopkins Press, p. 33, fn. 3.
3   Freedman, L. (1983) *The Evolution of Nuclear Strategy*, London, Macmillan, p. 139.
4   Ermarth, F.W. 'Contrasts in American and Soviet Strategic

Thought', in Leebaert, D. (ed.) (1981) *Soviet Military Thinking*, London, George Allen and Unwin, p. 56.

5 See MccGwire, M. 'The Rationale for the Development of Soviet Seapower', in Baylis, J. and Segal, G. (eds) (1981) *Soviet Strategy*, London, Croom Helm, p. 217.

6 Ermarth, in Leebaert (1981), p. 57.

7 Arnett, R.L. 'Soviet Attitudes Towards Nuclear War: Do They Really Think They Can Win?', in Baylis and Segal, (1981) p. 61.

8 See 'Debate over a Frozen Planet', *Time*, 24 December 1984, pp. 44–45.

9 See Freedman (1983), p. 195.

10 For instance, see Kissinger, H. (1957) *Nuclear Weapons and Foreign Policy*, New York, Harper; Osgood, R. (1957) *Limited War: The Challenge to American Strategy*, Chicago, University of Chicago Press; and Brodie, B. (1959) *Strategy in the Missile Age*, Princeton, New Jersey, Princeton University Press.

11 For a concise discussion of Soviet thinking on limited war in Europe in the 1950s and 1960s, see Wolfe (1970), pp. 208–216.

12 Sienkiewicz, S., 'Soviet Nuclear Doctrine and the Prospects for Strategic Arms Control', in Leebaert (1981), pp. 76–77. For further discussion of this ambiguity, see Ermarth, in Leebaert (1981), pp. 61–62.

13 For an excellent and highly acclaimed analysis, see Ball, D. (1981) *Can Nuclear War Be Controlled?*, Adelphi Paper 169, London, IISS.

14 Ibid., p. 35.

15 See Holloway, D. (1984) *The Soviet Union and the Arms Race* , New Haven and London, Yale University Press, pp. 31–32.

16 Williams, P. 'Deterrence', in Baylis, J., Booth, K., Garnett, J. and Williams, P. (1975) *Contemporary Strategy. Theories and Policies*, London, Croom Helm, p. 69. Williams' chapter provides a lucid and concise analysis of the characteristics, requirements and problems of deterrence in the contemporary world.

17 From a speech by John Foster Dulles, quoted in Freedman (1983), p. 85.

18 Quoted in Freedman (1983), p. 87.

19 Halperin, M. (1972) *Contemporary Military Strategy*, London, Faber and Faber, p. 109.

20 See Holloway (1984), p. 32.

21 Erickson, J. (1982) 'The Soviet View of Deterrence: A General Survey', *Survival*, Vol. XXIV, No. 6, November/December 1982, p. 245.

22 Ibid., p. 244.

23 Quoted in Holloway (1984), p. 32.
24 Ibid., p. 34.
25 See Erickson (1982), p. 244.
26 Holloway (1984), p. 55.
27 Drell, S., Farley, P. and Holloway, D. (1984) 'Preserving the ABM Treaty', *International Security*, Vol. 9, No. 2, Fall 1984, p. 89. For two other highly critical analyses of SDI, see Bundy, McG., Kennan, G., McNamara, R. and Smith, G. (1984) 'The President's Choice: Star Wars or Arms Control', *Foreign Affairs*, Vol. 63, No. 2, Winter 1984/85, pp. 264–278, and Glaser, C. (1984) 'Why Even Good Defenses May Be Bad', *International Security*, Vol. 9, No. 2, Fall 1984, pp. 92–123. For arguments supportive of SDI, see Gray, C. (1985) 'A Case for Strategic Defence', *Survival*, Vol. XXVII, No. 2, March/April 1985, pp. 50–55, and Payne, K. and Gray, C. (1984) 'Nuclear Policy and the Defensive Transition', *Foreign Affairs*, Vol. 62, No. 4, Spring 1984, pp. 820–842.
28 See Spanier, J. (1972) *Games Nations Play*, London, Nelson, pp. 241–242.
29 Ibid., p. 242.
30 See Garthoff, R. 'Mutual Deterrence, Parity and Strategic Arms Limitations in Soviet Policy', in Leebaert (1981), pp. 92–124, especially pp. 112–121.
31 Blechman, B. and Hart, D. (1982) 'The Political Utility of Nuclear Weapons: The 1973 Middle East Crisis', *International Security*, Vol. 7, No. 1, Summer 1982, p. 152. Other excellent analyses and surveys of the crisis are to be found in Bell, C. (1977) *The Diplomacy of Détente*, London, Martin Robertson, Chap. 5; Kissinger, H. (1982) *Years of Upheaval*, London, Weidenfeld and Nicolson and Michael Joseph; and Jonsson, C. (1984) *Superpower*, London, Frances Pinter, pp. 171–191.
32 See Bjol, E. (1983) *Nordic Security*, Adelphi Paper 181, London, IISS.

CHAPTER 4 GEOPOLITICAL ACCOMMODATION

1 See Windsor, P. 'Stability and Instability in Eastern Europe and their Implications for Western Policy', in Dawisha, K. and Hanson, P. (eds) (1981) *Soviet–East European Dilemmas*, London, Heinemann, p. 202.
2 Korbonski, A. 'Soviet Policy towards Poland', in Terry, S.A. (ed.) (1984) *Soviet Policy in East Europe*, New Haven and London, Yale University Press, pp. 85–86.

3   Larrabbee, F.S. 'Soviet Crisis Management in Eastern Europe', in Holloway, D. and Sharp, J. (eds) (1984) *The Warsaw Pact – Alliance in Transition?*, London, Macmillan, p. 131.
4   Hanreider, W.F. and Auton, G.P. (1980) *The Foreign Policies of West Germany, France and Britain*, Englewood Cliffs, New Jersey, Prentice-Hall Inc., p. 56.
5   See Windsor, P. (1969) *German Reunification*, London, Elek, p. 126.
6   Brandt, W. (1978) *People and Politics*, London, Collins, p. 19.
7   See Whetten, L.W. (1971) *Germany's Ostpolitik*, London, Oxford University Press, p. 15.
8   Ibid., p. 39.
9   Ibid., p. 72.
10 See Morgan, R. (1974) *The United States and West Germany 1945–1973*, London, Oxford University Press, pp. 186–187.
11 De Porte, A.W. (1979) *Europe Between the Superpowers*, New Haven and London, Yale University Press, p. 184.
12 Morgan (1974), p. 187.
13 See Hanreider and Auton (1980), p. 68.
14 See Brandt (1978), p. 333.
15 Ibid., p. 332.
16 See Whetten (1971), p. 157.
17 Ibid., p. 158.
18 For a fascinating insight into, and details of, the difficulties encountered, see Brandt (1978), Chap. 14, pp. 366–397.
19 Ibid., p. 367.
20 Ulam, A. (1974) *Expansion and Coexistence*, New York, Praeger, p. 755.
21 Brandt (1978), p. 391.
22 Ibid., pp. 416–418.
23 Joffe, J. (1980) 'All Quiet on the Eastern Front', *Foreign Policy 37*, Winter 1979/80, p. 164.
24 For data on West German–East European trade, see Stern, F. (1980) 'Germany In a Semi-Gaullist Europe', *Foreign Affairs*, Vol. 58, No. 4, Spring 1980, pp. 880–881.
25 See Joffe (1980), p. 167.
26 Brandt (1978), p. 392.
27 See Joffe (1980), pp. 161–163.
28 See De Porte (1979), p. 178.
29 For the political background to the CSCE, see Buchan, A. (1974) *The End of the Postwar Era*, London, Weidenfeld and Nicolson, pp. 50–52. For details of the Brezhnev Doctrine, see Edmonds, R. (1977) *Soviet Foreign Policy 1962-1973*, London, Oxford University Press, pp. 73–74,

30 For a concise and somewhat cynical – perhaps realistic – appreciation of the three 'Baskets' of the CSCE, see Ulam, A. (1984) *Dangerous Relations*, New York, Oxford University Press, pp. 141–144.

31 Hoffmann, S. (1980) *Primacy or World Order*, New York, McGraw-Hill, p. 55.

32 See Brandt (1978), p. 426.

33 See Ulam (1984), p. 143.

34 See 'Conference on Security and Cooperation in Europe, Final Act, 1 August 1975', reprinted in *Survival*, Vol. XVII, No.6, November/December 1975, p. 297.

35 Sherer Jr., A.W. (1980) 'Goldberg's Variation', *Foreign Policy 39*, Summer 1980, p. 155.

36 Andelman, D.A. (1980) 'The Road to Madrid', *Foreign Policy 39*, Summer 1980, p. 163.

37 Hoffmann (1980), p. 291.

38 See Gaddis, J.L. (1982) *Strategies of Containment*, Oxford, Oxford University Press, p. 319.

39 See Brown, S. (1983) *The Faces of Power*, New York, Columbia University Press, pp. 332–333.

40 Ibid., pp. 469–470.

41 See 'Words versus deeds', *Economist*, 31 January 1981, pp. 42–43.

42 See Brandon, H. (1982) 'The fog of illusion obscuring a viable approach to Madrid', *Sunday Times*, 24 October 1982, p. 21, and Jackson, H. (1982) 'The return of the talking blocs', *Guardian*, 9 November 1982, p. 15.

43 Quoted in Mather, I. (1984) 'Schultz and Gromyko may breathe life into *détente*', *Observer*, 15 January, 1984, p. 7.

44 Goodby, J. (1984) 'Security for Europe', *NATO Review*, No. 3, June 1984, p. 9.

45 Ibid., p. 11.

46. See Mather I. (1984) 'Schultz and Gromyko may breathe ife into *détente*', *Observer*, 15 January 1984, p. 7.

47 For the full range of NATO proposals of January 1984, see Goodby (1984), p. 12.

48 For information and analysis of progress of MFR talks since 1973, see *Strategic Survey*, London, IISS, published annually. There is normally an arms control chapter.

49 See *Statement of the Defence Estimates 1979*, Cmnd. 7474, London, HMSO, Chap. 1, pp. 3–4, paras 111–113.

50 For detailed discussion of the data problem, see Brady, L.P. (1981) 'Negotiating European Security: Mutual and Balanced Force

Reductions', *International Security Review*, Vol. 6, No. 2, Summer 1981, pp. 196–200.

51 See 'An East-Bloc Offer on MBFR', *Newsweek*, 18 March 1985, pp. 18–19.

52 Brady (1981), p. 191.

53 Bertram, C. (1972) *Mutual Force Reductions in Europe: The Political Aspects*, Adelphi Paper 84, London, IISS, p. 4.

CHAPTER 5 PROSPECTS

1 See Freedman, L. (1985) 'The "Star Wars" Debate: The Western Alliance and Strategic Defence: Part II', *New Technology and Western Security Policy Part III*, Adelphi Paper 199, London, IISS, p. 39.

2 For an interesting assessment of the effectiveness of non-Soviet Warsaw Pact armies in a NATO–Warsaw Pact conflict, see Herspring, D. and Volgyes, I. (1980) 'How Reliable Are East European Armies?', *Survival*, Vol. XXII, No. 5, September/October 1980, pp. 208–218.

3 See Sheehan, M. (1983) *The Arms Race*, Oxford, Martin Robertson, pp. 151–153.

4 For instance, see Greenwood, D. (1984) 'Strengthening Conventional Deterrence', *NATO Review*, No. 4, August 1984, pp. 8–12; Mather, I. (1984) 'Deep-strike NATO worries Bonn', *Observer*, 9 December 1984; Weinberger, C. (1984) 'Assessing Current NATO Strategy', *NATO's Sixteen Nations*, November/December 1984, pp. 38–41; and Rogers, B. (1984) 'Follow-on Forces Attack (FOFA): myths and realities', *NATO Review*, No. 6, December 1984, pp. 1-9.

5 For instance, see Bundy McG., Kennan, G., McNamara, R, and Smith, G. (1982) 'Nuclear Weapons and the Atlantic Alliance', *Foreign Affairs*, Vol. 60, No. 4, Spring 1982, pp. 753–768; and *No first use. A report by the Union of Concerned Scientists*, Cambridge, Mass., February 1983.

6 For instance, see Kaiser, K., Leber, G., Mertes, A., and Schulze, F.-J. (1982) 'Nuclear Weapons and the Preservation of Peace', *Foreign Affairs*, Vol. 60, No. 5, Summer 1982, pp. 1157–1170; Howard, M. (1982) 'The Issue of No First Use', letter to *Foreign Affairs*, Vol. 61, No. 1., Fall 1982, p. 211; and Critchley, J. (1982) 'Should the First Use of Nuclear Arms be Renounced?', *RUSIJ*, Vol. 127, No. 4, December 1982, pp. 32–34.

7 For instance, see Erickson, J. (1978) 'The European Military Balance', in Kirk, G. and Wessel, N. (eds) (1978) *The Soviet Threat. Myth and Realities*, New York, Praeger, pp. 110–121; Stanhope, H.

(1979) 'New Threat – or Old Fears?', in Leebaert, D. (ed.) (1979) *European Security: Prospects for the 1980s*, Lexington, Mass., Lexington Books, pp. 39–60; Mearsheimer, J. (1982) 'Why the Soviets Can't Win Quickly in Central Europe', *International Security*, Vol. 7, No. 4, Spring 1983, pp. 3-39; and 'The East–West Conventional Balance in Europe', *The Military Balance 1984–1985*, London, IISS, pp. 148–153.

8   Ibid., *The Military Balance*, p. 151.

9   See Defence and Overseas Policy Working Group of the British Atlantic Committee (1981) *A Global Strategy to Meet the Global Threat*, London, British Atlantic Committee; and the Directors of the Research Institute of the German Society for Foreign Policy, the Council on Foreign Relations (New York), the French Institute of International Relations, and the Royal Institute for International Affairs (1981) *Western Security: What has Changed? What Should be Done?*, London, RIIA.

10 See Maull, H. (1984) *Raw Materials, Energy and Western Security*, London, Macmillan, for a much acclaimed, non-alarmist analysis of the resource vulnerability of the West.

11 Posen, B. and Van Evera, S. (1983) 'Defense Policy and the Reagan Administration: Departure from Containment', *International Security*, Vol. 8, No. 1, Summer 1983, p. 33.

12 For arguments that alliances are more liable to fissure the greater their scope, see Morgenthau, H. (1959) 'Alliances in theory and practice', in Wolfers, A. (ed.) (1959) *Alliance Policy in the Cold War*, Baltimore, Johns Hopkins Press, pp. 184–212; and Dinerstein, H. (1965) 'Transformation of alliance systems', *American Political Science Review*, Vol. 59, No. 3, September 1965, pp. 589–601.

13 For a detailed and comprehensive review of current French defence policy see Yost, D. (1985) *France's Deterrent Posture and Security in Europe Parts I and II*, Adelphi Papers 194 and 195, London, IISS.

14 See Greenwood (1984a), pp. 10–12, and Greenwood, D. (1984) 'Reshaping NATO's defences', *Defence Minister and Chief of Staff*, No. 5, 1984, pp. 9-19.

15 See Schopflin, G. (1981) 'The Political Structure of Eastern Europe as a factor in Intra-bloc Relations', in Dawisha, K. and Hanson, P. (eds) (1981) *Soviet-East European Dilemmas*, London, Heinemann, pp. 64–66; and 'Testing the Kremlin's Limits', *Newsweek*, 29 October 1984, pp. 8-12.

16 See Azmus, R. (1983) 'Is There a Peace Movement in the GDR?', *Orbis*, Vol. 27, No. 2, Summer 1983, pp. 301–341; and English, R.

(1984) 'Eastern Europe's Doves', *Foreign Policy 56*, Fall 1984, pp. 44–60.

17   See *Strategic Survey 1984–1985*, London, IISS, pp. 52–55.
18   See Schopflin in Dawisha and Hanson (1981), pp. 66–72.
19   See Treverton, G. (1984) 'Economics and Security in the Atlantic Alliance', *Survival*, Vol. XXVI, No. 6, November/December 1984, p. 269.
20   Ibid., p. 277.

Select Bibliography

Ambrose, S. E. (1973) *Rise to Globalism*, Harmondsworth, Penguin.

Aron, R. (1965) *The Century of Total War*, Boston, Beacon Press.

Aron, R. (1974) *The Imperial Republic*, London, Weidenfeld and Nicolson.

Ball, D. (1981) *Can Nuclear War Be Controlled?*, Adelphi Paper 169, London, IISS.

Barnet, R.J. (1972) *Intervention and Revolution*, London, Paladin.

Baylis, J. and Segal, G. (eds) (1981) *Soviet Strategy*, London, Croom Helm.

Bell, C. (1977) *The Diplomacy of Detente*, London, Martin Robertson.

Bond, B. (1984) *War and Society in Europe 1870–1970*, London, Fontana.

Boutwell, J. (1983) 'Politics and the Peace Movement in West Germany', *International Security*, Vol. 7, No. 4, Spring 1983, pp. 72–92.

Brady, L.P. (1981) 'Negotiating European Security: Mutual and Balanced Force Reductions', *International Security Review*, Vol. 6, No. 2, Summer 1981, pp. 189–208.

Brandt, W. (1978) *People and Politics*, London, Collins.

Brown, S. (1983) *The Faces of Power*, New York, Columbia University Press.

Buchan, A. (1974) *The End of the Postwar Era*, London, Weidenfeld and Nicolson.

Bundy, McG., Kennan, G., McNamara, R. and Smith, G. (1982) 'Nuclear Weapons and the Atlantic Alliance', *Foreign Affairs*, Vol. 60, No. 4, Spring 1982, pp. 753–768.

Bundy, McG., Kennan, G., McNamara, R., and Smith, G. (1984) 'The President's Choice: Star Wars or Arms Control', *Foreign Affairs*, Vol. 63, No. 2, Winter 1984/85, pp. 264–278.

Clemens, D.S. (1972) *YALTA*, London, Oxford University Press.

Dawisha, K. and Hanson, P. (eds) (1981) *Soviet–East European Dilemmas*, London, Heinemann.

De Porte, A.W. (1979) *Europe Between the Superpowers*, New Haven and London, Yale University Press.

Drell, S., Farley, P., and Holloway, D. (1984) 'Preserving the ABM Treaty', *International Security*, Vol. 9, No. 2, Fall 1984, pp. 51–91.

Edmonds, R. (1977) *Soviet Foreign Policy 1962–1973*, London, Oxford University Press.

English, R. (1984) 'Eastern Europe's Doves', *Foreign Policy 56*, Fall 1984, pp. 44–60.

Erickson, J. (1982) 'The Soviet View of Deterrence: A General Survey', *Survival*, Vol. XXIV, No. 6, November/December 1982, pp. 242–251.

Feis, H. (1970) *From Trust to Terror*, London, Antony Blond.

Freedman, L. (1981) 'NATO Myths', *Foreign Policy 45*, Winter 1981/82, pp. 48–68.

Freedman, L. (1982a) 'Limited War, Unlimited Protest', *Orbis*, Vol. 26, No. 1, Spring 1982, pp. 89–103.

Freedman, L. (1983) *The Evolution of Nuclear Strategy*, London, Macmillan.

Freedman, L. (1985) 'The "Star Wars" Debate: The Western Alliance and Strategic Defence: Part II', *New Technology and Western Security Policy Part III*, Adelphi Paper 199, London, IISS, pp. 34–50.

Gaddis, J.L. (1982) *Strategies of Containment*, Oxford, Oxford University Press.

Goodby, J. (1984) 'Security for Europe', *NATO Review*, No. 3, June 1984, pp. 9–14.

Gray, C. (1985) 'A Case for Strategic Defence', *Survival*, Vol. XXVII, No. 2, March/April 1985, pp. 50–55.

Greenwood, D. (1984a) 'Strengthening Conventional Deterrence', *NATO Review*, No. 4, August 1984, pp. 8–12.

Griffith, W.E. (1982) 'Bonn and Washington: From Deterioration to Crisis?', *Orbis*, Vol. 26, No. 1, Spring 1982, pp. 117–133.

Halle, L.J. (1967) *The Cold War As History*, London, Chatto and Windus.

Halperin, M. (1982) 'NATO and the TNF Controversy: Threats to the Alliance', *Orbis*, Vol. 26, No. 1, Spring 1982, pp. 105–116.

Hanreider, W.F. and Auton, G.P. (1980) *The Foreign Policies of West Germany, France and Britain*, Englewood Cliffs, New Jersey, Prentice-Hall Inc.

Hoffman, S. (1980) *Primacy or World Order*, New York, McGraw-Hill.

Hoffmann, E.P. and Fleron, F.J. (eds) (1980) *The Conduct of Soviet Foreign Policy*, New York, Aldine Publishing Co.

Holloway, D. (1984)   *The Soviet Union and the Arms Race*, New Haven and London, Yale University Press.

Holloway, D. and Sharp, J. (eds) (1984)   *The Warsaw Pact – Alliance in Transition?*, London, Macmillan.

Howard, M. (1983)   'Deterrence, Consensus and Reassurance in the Defence of Europe', *Defence and Consensus: The Domestic Aspects of Western Security, Part III*, Adelphi Paper 184, London, IISS, pp. 17–26.

Hunter, R. (1972)   *Security in Europe*, London, Paul Elek.

IISS   *Strategic Survey*, London, IISS, published annually.

IISS   *The Military Balance*, London, IISS, published annually.

Joffe, J. (1980)   'All Quiet on the Eastern Front', *Foreign Policy 37*, Winter 1979/80, pp. 161–172.

Kaiser, K., Leber, G., Mertes, A., and Schulze, F.-J. (1982)   'Nuclear Weapons and the Preservation of Peace' *Foreign Affairs*, Vol. 60, No. 5, Summer 1982, pp. 1157–1170.

Kennan, G. (1967)   *Memoirs 1925–1950*, Boston, Little, Brown and Co.

Kissinger, H. (1979)   *The White House Years*, London, Weidenfeld and Nicolson and Michael Joseph.

Kissinger, H. (1982)   *Years of Upheaval*, London, Weidenfeld and Nicolson and Michael Joseph.

Leebaert, D. (ed.) (1979)   *European Security: Prospects for the 1980s*, Lexington, Mass., Lexington Books.

Leebaert, D. (ed.) (1981)   *Soviet Military Thinking*, London, George Allen and Unwin.

Mackintosh, M. (1969)   *The Evolution of the Warsaw Pact*, Adelphi Paper 58, London, IISS.

Mandelbaum, M. (1981)   *The Nuclear Revolution*, Cambridge, Cambridge University Press.

Mastny, V. (1979)   *Russia's Road to the Cold War*, New York, Columbia University Press.

Maull, H. (1984)   *Raw Materials, Energy and Western Security*, London, Macmillan.

Moreton, E. and Segal, G. (1984)   *Soviet Strategy Toward West Europe*, London, George Allen and Unwin.

Morgan, R. (1974)   *The United States and West Germany 1945–1973*, London, Oxford University Press.

Nogee, J.L. and Donaldson, R.H. (1981)   *Soviet Foreign Policy Since World War II*, New York, Pergamon Press.

Osgood, R. (1966)   *NATO: The Entangling Alliance*, Chicago and London, University of Chicago Press.

Posen, B. and Van Evera, S. (1983)   'Defense Policy and the Reagan

Administration: Departure from Containment', *International Security*, Vol. 8, No. 1, Summer 1983, pp. 3–43.

Rees, D. (1971)   *The Age of Containment*, London, Macmillan.

Schlesinger Jr., A. (1967)   'Origins of the Cold War', *Foreign Affairs*, Vol. 46, No. 1, October 1967, pp. 22–52.

Segal, G., Moreton, E., Freedman, L., and Baylis, J. (1983)   *Nuclear War and Nuclear Peace*, London, Macmillan.

Sheehan, M. (1983)   *The Arms Race*, Oxford, Martin Robertson.

Spanier, J. (1972)   *Games Nations Play*, London, Nelson.

Spanier, J. (1972)   *American Foreign Policy since World War II*, London, Nelson.

Steele, J. (1983)   *World Power*, London, Michael Joseph.

Terry, S.A. (ed.) (1984)   *Soviet Policy in East Europe*, New Haven and London, Yale University Press.

Thomson, D. (1967)   *Europe Since Napoleon*, Harmondsworth, Penguin.

Treverton, G. (1981)   *Nuclear Weapons in Europe*, Adelphi Paper 168, London, IISS.

Ulam, A.B. (1974)   *Expansion and Coexistence*, New York, Praeger.

Ulam, A.B. (1984)   *Dangerous Relations*, New York, Oxford University Press.

van Voorst, L. Bruce (1982)   'The Critical Masses', *Foreign Policy 48*, Fall 1982, pp. 82–93.

Whetten, L.W. (1971)   *Germany's Ostpolitik*, London, Oxford University Press.

Windsor, P. (1969)   *German Reunification*, London, Elek.

Wolfe, T.W. (1970)   *Soviet Power and Europe 1945–1970*, Baltimore, Johns Hopkins Press.

Yergin, D. (1980)   *The Shattered Peace*, Harmondsworth, Penguin.

Index